ALSO BY RABBI ABNER WEISS, PH.D.

Death and Bereavement: A Halakhic Guide to Mourning

Rabbis as Mental Health Professionals

CONNECTING TO GOD

ANCIENT KABBALAH AND
MODERN PSYCHOLOGY

RABBI ABNER WEISS, PH.D.

BELL TOWER

NEW YORK

Grateful acknowledgment is made to the following for permission to reprint previously published material:

Jason Aronson: Excerpts from *The Holy Letter,* by Nahmanides, translated by Seymour J. Cohen. Copyright © 1993, 1976 by Seymour J. Cohen. Reprinted by permission of Jason Aronson, an imprint of Rowman & Littlefield Publishers, Inc., Lanham, Maryland.

Vallentine, Mitchell & Co., Ltd.: Excerpts from *The Palm Tree of Deborah,* by Rabbi Moses Cordovero, translated by Louis Jacobs. Copyright © 1960 by Louis Jacobs. Reprinted by permission of Vallentine, Mitchell & Co., Ltd.

Published in the United States by Bell Tower, an imprint of the Crown Publishing Group, a division of Random House, Inc., New York.
www.crownpublishing.com

Bell Tower and colophon are registered trademarks of Random House, Inc.

Library of Congress Cataloging-in-Publication Data
Weiss, Abner.
    Connecting to God : ancient kabbalah and modern psychology / Abner Weiss.—1st ed.
    Includes bibliographical references and index.
    1. Psychotherapy—Religious aspects—Judaism.   2. Cabala—Psychology.
    3. Reincarnation therapy.   4. Meditation—Judaism.   5. Psychotherapy patients—
    Anecdotes.   I. Title.
    BM538.P68W45 2005
    296.3'71—dc22   2004030719

ISBN 1-4000-8334-6

Printed in the United States of America

Design by Meryl Sussman Levavi

10 9 8 7 6 5 4 3 2 1

First Edition

For my dear friends
Dawn and Roland Arnall,
and
my beloved wife, Dr. Yolande Bloomstein

ACKNOWLEDGMENTS

After hearing my lecture on ancient Kabbalah and modern psychology, Roland and Dawn Arnall urged me to expand my talk into a book. They have helped me to complete this project in myriad ways. I shall forever be grateful to them for their love and friendship.

Dr. Yolande Bloomstein is my beloved wife and my partner in our mental health practice. Her support, encouragement, inspiration, and sound judgment have added immeasurably to the quality of this book.

I am also grateful to the participants in the workshops that I cofacilitated with the late Dr. Harry Jakobs, and to the clients who were open to my using the techniques described in the book as part of their therapeutic regimen. To paraphrase an old rabbinic dictum: I have learned much from my teachers but even more from my clients.

My collaboration with Toinette Lippe at Bell Tower has been enriching in many ways. She has taught me just how important a gifted editor is in the creation of a good book and has improved and tightened my writing, making the book infinitely more readable. Her charm and grace have turned a technical collaborator into a valued friend. My copy editor, Jim Gullickson, was meticulous, and I am grateful to him for his contribution. I am particularly grateful to Jennifer Joel, my agent at International Creative Management, for the personal interest she has taken in this project.

I have been blessed with teachers, colleagues, and friends who have spent a great deal of time reading and critiquing the manuscript. I am particularly grateful to Dr. Stanley Krippner, professor of psychology at my alma mater, Saybrook Graduate School and Research Center, who commented on almost every page of the manuscript, correcting errors of fact and interpretation, directing me to studies of which I was not aware, and helping me to define and articulate psychological concepts in accessible language. Ron West not only brought his critical acumen to bear on the shaping of the book, but also helped keep the project moving. Our friend Beverly Miller of London shared copious comments with me by e-mail and enhanced the text in many ways. In an inspired moment, my brother-in-law, Henry Bloomstein, provided the title of the book. Dr. Mark Cohen, himself a published author on the Kabbalah, read the manuscript painstakingly and made valuable suggestions that were incorporated into the book. Rabbi David Wolpe's comments were also very helpful. I could not have wished for better proofreaders than Shep Drazin, Michael Goland, Hanita Hoffman, Ken Klee, Stephanie Levi, and Erma Oppenheim. Nancy Abrams, my personal assistant on this project, encouraged me when I seemed stuck and did not let me get away with either sloppy thinking or careless writing. I have been fortunate to have her work with me during these past two years.

Jerry Rosenbloom is the president of my very special congregation, the Westwood Village Synagogue, whose members have welcomed Yolande and me into their homes and hearts. Jerry's extraordinary talents as a graphic designer are evidenced by the beautiful illustrations he has created for this book.

CONTENTS

LIST OF ILLUSTRATIONS

PREFACE

The **Kabbalah*** is the Jewish mystic way, but you don't have to be Jewish to benefit from this book. Nor do you have to know a word of Hebrew or Aramaic, the original languages of kabbalistic literature, to understand its ancient secrets. You simply need to have a thirst for the truth and be a sincere seeker of life's meaning and purposes.

For centuries, the study of Kabbalah was mainly esoteric, hermetic, theological, and intellectual. Now you can also profit from its practical, therapeutic, and transformational wisdom. Not too long ago, the wisdom of the Kabbalah was one of humankind's best-kept secrets. Its texts were extremely difficult to understand, and were closely guarded by generation after generation of elite spiritual masters and their small groups of students.

However, about twenty years ago, an enormous change took place, and there was a universal upsurge of interest in the Kabbalah. Books on the subject began to appear in astonishing numbers. Thousands of people throughout the world flocked to lectures. The lives of spiritual seekers of all backgrounds were changed by exposure to kabbalistic teachings and practices. Most of these were ordinary people. Some were high-profile individuals, whose lives were dramatically improved by their study of this

*Terms in bold can be found in the glossary at the back of the book.

xiii

ancient wisdom. Jewish icons of pop culture, like Barbra Streisand and Roseanne Barr, have gone public about the benefits of Kabbalah. Non-Jewish devotees, like Madonna and Demi Moore, have helped make Kabbalah a household word.

To benefit from the practical, therapeutic wisdom of the Kabbalah, you must first become acquainted with the history of this ancient tradition. You must learn how it fits in with the rest of God's revelation, the way divine energy permeates the cosmos, the structure and the many journeys of the human soul, and the nature of the Tree of Life. Then you will discover how to apply the principles of Kabbalah to your own life. I have done my best to present difficult concepts in a simple way, without sacrificing the integrity of the marvelous kabbalistic system.

The human soul is hardwired to channel divine energy into thinking, feeling, relating, and being in the world. However, this mechanism can be thrown out of balance by our experiences in previous lives and what happens to us in this lifetime. This book describes ways to restore your psychospiritual balance and reenergize the way you think, feel, and relate. It tells twenty-eight stories of individuals, couples, and families who used kabbalistic exercises together with the clinically tested strategies of contemporary psychologists to liberate themselves from their self-defeating ways of being. As you read this book, you will learn how these interventions healed and transformed them, and how they can help you, too.

Since I am to be your guide on this journey, it is only fair that you get to know me. I began to meditate when I was a teenager in Johannesburg, South Africa, although I had never read a book on meditation nor met any teachers of the contemplative way. Something inspired me to quiet my mind for fifteen or twenty minutes each day and travel as deeply into myself as I could. At the same time, I devoured every book on the occult in the local public library and began to study the writings of the masters of the Eastern mystical traditions.

In addition, my experience at Sabbath services in our small neighborhood synagogue began to startle me. I became aware of an unfamiliar excitement while reciting some of the prayers. At times, this excitement produced physical changes. I noticed that I was covered with goose bumps when I felt particularly connected to God. So I began to turn to works on Jewish spirituality for further enlightenment. To my surprise, I discovered that the truths for which I had been searching in other mystical traditions were an important part of my own heritage. Sadly, Jewish mysticism had never been mentioned by my teachers in religious school. It was not even part of the curriculum in most higher institutes of Jewish learning.

At that time, I had no plans to become a rabbi. I had become deeply interested in psychology and had considered making counseling my career. However, I was turned off by the prevalent anti-spiritual bias of most academic psychologists. Then, at about the same time as Kabbalah entered the spiritual mainstream, psychology recovered its soul. This change eventually encouraged me to pursue graduate studies leading to a Ph.D. in psychology and licensure as a marriage and family therapist. However, I still did not at that time recognize the connection between my twin passions, ancient Kabbalah and contemporary psychology.

A 1995 lecture by noted psychiatrist Brian Weiss (unfortunately, not a relation) in my synagogue in Beverly Hills, California, catalyzed my explorations. Dr. Weiss had had no previous knowledge of Jewish spirituality. His perfunctory Jewish education had not prepared him for what he would accidentally discover. He had been attempting to help one of his patients overcome her debilitating fear of swallowing. None of the usual interventions had provided relief, and so he decided to regress her hypnotically further and further into her childhood and infancy as he sought the source of the trauma. To Weiss's astonishment, she regressed to a previous lifetime in which she had died by drowning. When she understood that her fear of swallowing was unrelated to her present lifetime, her phobia disappeared.

Once I heard Brian Weiss speak, I read his best-selling *Many Lives, Many Masters* and his other books on past-life regression. I also read everything else on that subject that was available. I had always known that the influence of past-life events on our current life experiences was a fundamental kabbalistic doctrine, and psychiatry had finally validated this ancient psychological secret. I also noted how famous psychiatrists, like Carl Jung and Roberto Assagioli, had described phenomena that were commonplace in the Kabbalah. The link between the ancient mystical tradition and contemporary psychology was becoming clearer and clearer, and so I decided to investigate it more rigorously.

As the kabbalistic theory of human nature, personality, and relationships became more evident to me, I decided to test it in practice. Initially, I used what I had discovered for my own psychospiritual growth, and my life improved dramatically. Then, in 1997, I cofacilitated a number of three-day workshops with a colleague. Some of the people who enrolled in the workshops had had serious emotional and relationship problems. Many were struggling with questions about the meaning and purpose of their lives and work. A goodly number were seeking a clearer understanding of who they were. Almost all had had psychotherapy for months, and even years. Nobody who participated was completely happy with life. The feedback from participants was exceedingly positive. Many people reported gaining fresh insights and experiencing psychospiritual breakthroughs. Very few failed to get something important from their experience. The therapeutic value of the Kabbalah was further confirmed for me in my private counseling practice, and so I decided to share my experience with larger audiences by lecturing in major cities in North America and Great Britain. As a consequence, both mental health professionals and laypeople urged me to publish what I had been teaching, and this book is the result.

ABNER WEISS
Los Angeles, California

1

PSYCHOLOGY AND SPIRITUALITY:
THE BRIDGE

THE FAILURE OF
THE PSYCHOLOGICAL REVOLUTION

A century of clinical psychology has made therapy a household concept in the Western world. More people than ever before have experienced psychotherapy. More methods for achieving psychological well-being are available. Miracle drugs alleviate depression and relieve anxiety. Gadgets of every description make household chores and business administration less tedious and more efficient. More time is available for relaxation, entertainment, continuing education, and personal growth.

These advances should have produced a happier and more fulfilled generation. But people seem to be no less troubled and no more relaxed and fulfilled than they were prior to the psychological revolution. What has gone wrong?

What happened to Sheila, Jeremy, and their extended family helps answer this question.

SHEILA AND JEREMY'S STORY

Our synagogue was launching an ambitious outreach program. We thought that High Holy Day services for young adult "beginners," with lots of explanations and opportunities for asking questions, might be a good way of attracting people who had been turned off or never turned on. In addition, we were offering home hospitality.

I received a call from a young man asking if he and his friend could spend the High Holy Days as my houseguests. This was the beginning of an experience that would prove to be transformative in more ways than I could imagine at the time.

Jeremy and Sheila arrived a few hours before the evening service. I learned that Jeremy was a professor at a local university, and that Sheila had been his student in another city. They had begun to talk about building a future together, and religion was the only issue that seriously troubled them.

Jeremy was Jewish by birth, but was an atheist. Both his parents were mental health professionals, and he had embraced their contempt for religion. His father was a professor of psychiatry with an international reputation for his research and clinical skills. His mother was a licensed clinical social worker who taught at the same university as her husband. Jeremy's father had been trained in Vienna before the Second World War, and had been persuaded by Sigmund Freud's *The Future of an Illusion* that religion was a collective neurosis. He was convinced that God did not exist and that the concept of the Divine was a human invention to serve social and psychological needs. Jeremy's mother shared her husband's beliefs. There were no Jewish observances or even Jewish symbols in their home. I was not surprised to learn that Jeremy had had no Jewish religious education.

Sheila, on the other hand, came from a religious home. Her parents were sincere believers and had given their children a solid Christian education, but Sheila had some reservations about religion. The threat of hellfire and damnation for religious noncompliance and the negative attitude to other faiths by the family pastor troubled her deeply. However, she knew that her life needed to be spiritually centered and wanted to find an alternative to the religious values and experiences she had encountered.

Jeremy had tried to persuade Sheila that her quest for spirituality made no sense, but she told him that it was a vital part of her being. She pointed out that Jeremy had never been exposed to religion and suggested that his rejection of something he had not experienced was unreasonable. Jeremy reluctantly agreed to give religion a try. Sheila thought that Unitarian Christianity might be less objectionable to Jeremy than the Christianity of her childhood. She hoped, too, that it would do something for her. So Jeremy and Sheila had attended services at a Unitarian church near the university, but left uninspired. Then she had suggested that they go to services at a Reform Jewish temple. The services in that ultraliberal synagogue did not seem very different from the disappointing worship experience in the Unitarian church. It was at that point that the couple had relocated to our city.

Jeremy and Sheila were moved by their High Holy Day experience and decided to attend the beginners' service on a weekly basis. Sheila asked me for literature on Judaism. She was an avid reader and devoured every book I recommended. Jeremy spent many hours in the library reading up on Judaism and confided to me that he had discovered hidden hungers. After about six months, they came to see me about Sheila's converting to Judaism. I told them that they would both need to take classes and become involved in the other spiritual activities of the community. They were ready to do so and enrolled in the conversion program. They continued to read voraciously, mastered Hebrew, and made changes in their lifestyle that reflected their growing religious commitment.

Shortly before Sheila's conversion, I asked them about their wedding plans. They said that they wanted to marry as soon after the conversion as possible, but that their wedding plans had brought Jeremy into open conflict with his parents. His parents approved of Sheila, but resisted the couple's request that their wedding be catered kosher. They felt it was a rejection of their beliefs and of the way they had brought up their son. They saw me as the villain responsible for undermining everything they had done to disabuse their son of religious superstition. To put it mildly, they detested me.

However, a kosher wedding was eventually held and Jeremy's parents attended reluctantly. Over the next few years, Jeremy and Sheila had children and introduced them to the beauty of Jewish practice. I had no contact with them for several years. Then, one day, I received a phone call. "Rabbi," a voice said tentatively, "do you remember me?" It was Jeremy. "I need to ask you a huge favor," he said. "My dad has a brain tumor. He wants you to come and see him in the hospital."

All kinds of thoughts raced through my head, mainly that the old psychiatrist was finally going to let me have it for ruining his son and his grandchildren. I thought it was one of the last issues he needed to tie up before he died. Somewhat nervously, I asked, "When would he like to see me?"

"How about tonight?" Jeremy replied.

That evening, prayer book clasped in hand (perhaps more to comfort me than him), I knocked on his father's door. A German-accented voice invited me in. We were alone in the room. "You asked to see me," I said.

He fixed his gaze on me. "Is it okay for an old man to say he's been a fool?" he asked. I could not believe what I was hearing. What did he mean? He answered my question before I asked it. "You know who I am, what I teach, and what I have believed. I was trained in Vienna. In high school we used to mock the rabbi whose classes we had to attend later in the day." He mimicked the rabbi's eastern European accent.

"*Mi-she-bayrach, Mi-she-bayrach, Mi-she-bayrach.* We thought this was a witch's incantation. After all, everything Jewish was supposed to be crude and primitive. These feelings were reinforced at medical school and became central to my beliefs. That's why I so bitterly resented your influence on my son."

"What happened?" I asked. "What made you think you've been wrong all these years?"

"Spirituality did not fit any of the accepted categories of the life and mental health sciences," he told me. "but I finally did discover spirituality at the Sabbath table in my son's home. The prayers and hymns resonated with a part of my soul I had completely disowned, and the radiance in the faces of my grandchildren transported me to another dimension."

"What happened after you made this discovery?" I asked.

"I decided that I needed to learn more. I began by asking my son to tell me what *Mi-she-bayrach* means."

"What did your son tell you?" I asked.

"He told me that *Mi-she-bayrach* is the beginning of an ancient Jewish prayer for blessing and healing," he answered. "And I've another confession. I have been attending your public lectures over the past few years."

"I did not know . . . ," I began.

"How could you? I did not introduce myself. I was not sure you would want to know me after what you had heard about me."

"Nothing would have given me more joy than to hear of your personal transformation," I replied.

"You're probably wondering why I wanted to see you," the old man said. "It was not only to tell you I had been a fool, and a very stubborn fool, at that. It was to ask you to do something for me. I'm about to have surgery to remove my brain tumor. Would you say a *Mi-she-bayrach* for me?"

This story is a dramatic illustration of the failure of the psychological revolution. The hidden hungers Jeremy had discovered pointed to an innate need for spirituality. Even the old Viennese professor had to admit that the traditional model was wrong, because it overlooked the universal yearning for spiritual fulfillment.

My first encounter with the study of psychology was in 1956. Six hundred freshmen were crowded into a large lecture hall at the University of the Witwatersrand in Johannesburg. None of us had any previous exposure to psychology. We were all eagerly awaiting the introductory session, which had been listed as "An Overview of the Science of Psychology." The instructor, a tall and very imposing man, wasted no time in laying all his cards on the table. "I'm going to disabuse you of three myths," he declared. "There is no God; there is no soul; and there is no mind. If you can get that archaic nonsense out of your heads, you'll be ready to study and practice psychology seriously."

Every undergraduate psychology course I took during the next several years proved his point. Experiences of transcendence and of spirituality were beyond the scope of psychology. Sigmund Freud had, after all, described himself as "the personal enemy of God." Spirituality was the problem, not the solution to people's problems. The psychiatric Bible is called *Diagnostic and Statistical Manual of Mental Disorders—DSM* for short. Therapists usually make their diagnoses according to *DSM* criteria. Until very recently, almost every reference to religion in the *DSM* was linked to pathology. Neurophysiology, learning theory, and experimental psychology had joined Freud in removing the soul from psychology.

Because God and soul were fundamental to my personal beliefs and way of life, I decided not to become a psychologist but to try another way of helping people to heal and grow. And so, after graduation, I enrolled at the local rabbinical seminary, eventually going to New York for my doctoral work on the writings of the great kabbalist Rabbi Judah Loewe of Prague (1512–1609). My study of his theory of psychology and ethics was my segue into the literature of the Kabbalah. At last, I had found my spiritual home.

After I received a Ph.D., I became a full-time rabbi. Kabbalah was still outside the bounds of mainstream Judaism, and the time was not yet right for me to publicly proclaim my kabbalistic convictions.

THE NEW PSYCHOLOGICAL REVOLUTION

Since then, there has been a huge paradigm shift in the field of psychology and, you will soon learn, in the attitude of the Jewish community to the Kabbalah. Not long before I met Jeremy and Sheila, I began to notice more and more books with "spirituality" in their titles in the psychology and self-help sections of good bookstores. Some of these books had become national best sellers.

Even the impact of the supernatural on psychological processes had been validated by the entry of transpersonal psychology into the mainstream. The transpersonal realm is the source of sudden flashes of blinding intuition and bursts of creativity. More and more researchers were addressing this phenomenon. Elmer Green of the renowned Menninger Clinic in Topeka, Kansas, had duplicated the experience in his laboratory following his physiological studies of yogis in India in 1974. His theta meditation techniques had opened his subjects not only to enhanced creativity but also to psychic experiences, such as clairvoyance and clairaudience.

I had long been convinced that intangible, metaphysical forces profoundly impact us physically as well as psychologically. In fact, members of most faith communities believe in the healing power of prayer. Let me share a remarkable story from my rabbinic notebook with you.

SAM'S STORY

One Sunday afternoon, while I was attending a wedding reception, my cell phone rang. "Rabbi," my caller said, "can you get to the hospital immediately?" I recognized the caller's voice, and, for a moment, I could not organize my thoughts. My questions simply tumbled out, one after the other. "What happened, Henya?" I asked. "Where are you? Which hospital shall I go to? Where will I find you?"

"Sam has had brain surgery. It was supposed to be minor, but something went terribly wrong. He is in a deep coma. I'll wait for you in the lobby of the medical center. How long will you be?"

"I should be there within fifteen minutes," I replied.

Once I had arrived, I tried unsuccessfully to elicit a response from her husband, but suggested that he might soon regain consciousness. I was wrong. He remained in a coma for two weeks, and then Henya asked me to put my faith on the line.

"Rabbi," she said, "Sam and I have been to hell and back. We survived the murder of our families, the massacre in our town, and Auschwitz. Only our faith kept us going. Don't take that away from me now. You have often told the congregation about the power of prayer. I ask you to prove it."

After a moment's hesitation, I promised to involve the congregation in a focused meditation and prayer for Sam's recovery. The next day was the Sabbath, and the synagogue was packed. About halfway through the service, I asked everybody to rise. I told them about Sam's condition and described the room he was in at the hospital. I asked them to picture him comatose in his hospital bed. I reminded them of the Jewish belief in the power of collective prayer and suggested that they send powerful healing thoughts to him. I could actually feel the spiritual energy that filled the sanctuary. We concluded our meditation with *Mi-she-bayrach,* the traditional prayer for recovery.

I confess that I was extremely nervous. I had never tried this before. What if our prayers failed to produce results? How would this affect the faith of the members of my congregation? I should not have worried. My telephone rang shortly after the conclusion of the Sabbath. It was Henya. She asked, "Rabbi, at exactly what time did you pray for Sam's recovery?"

"At about ten-forty this morning," I answered.

"It's amazing," she said. "Sam regained consciousness at precisely that time."

My relief was tangible, but it was also relatively short-lived. Sam lapsed into a coma again several days later. This time, however, Henya did not want to wait two weeks before asking for another spiritual intervention. The following Sabbath, I again asked the congregation to stand. We did exactly what we had done the week before. I was even more nervous. What if Sam's initial recovery had been a fluke? What would the people think if their prayer was unanswered this time? Nevertheless, I and the members of my synagogue prayed as hard as we could. Again, Sam regained consciousness at the time we were praying for him. But, unfortunately, after several days, he sank into a coma once more. I visited him while he was in this state. The neurosurgeon who was managing Sam's case happened to be in the room when I arrived. He showed me a beaker half filled with fluid. "Rabbi," he began, "do you see this fluid? I have just drained it from Sam's head. I've been draining this much fluid every day. I've seen the latest CAT scan. His brain is mush. There is no way he can recover. Please persuade his wife to let him go peacefully with no further intervention."

Unbeknownst to me, Henya had been standing in the hallway listening to our conversation. She burst into tears. "I will not listen to the doctor. I beg you to try prayer one last time."

The neurosurgeon looked at me skeptically. I gulped and said, "Doctor, please continue to do your thing, and let us try ours."

On the following Sabbath, I told the members of the synagogue exactly what had transpired with the neurosurgeon, and asked them to put everything they could into a final, powerful healing meditation for Sam.

The story had a very happy ending. For a third time, Sam regained consciousness at precisely the time we were praying for him, and, after a few weeks of rehabilitation, he returned home. Within a month, he was able to walk more than a mile to and from the synagogue each week. He did this for seven full years until he succumbed to the ravages of old age.

Our experience with Sam and others like him was ultimately validated by the scientific community. Larry Dossey, noted physician and author of *Healing Words,* confirmed the physical effects of distant healing. In a number of experiments, patients with the same condition and receiving identical traditional medical treatment were divided into two groups. The names and photographs of patients in one group were given to religious leaders. Each religious leader was given one name and one photograph and was asked to pray for the recovery of that patient. The studies were double-blind. None of the patients had any idea that they had been divided into two groups or that anybody was praying for some of them. The patients who were being prayed for did much better on all measures of health than those for whom nobody special was praying. Dossey's findings have been replicated by rigorous independent studies at prestigious medical centers. A systematic review of the studies on the efficacy of distant healing published in June

2000 in the *Annals of Internal Medicine* considered no fewer than twenty-three trials involving 2,774 patients. For example, a randomized, double-blind experiment was conducted by cardiologist Randolph Byrd over a ten-month period in 1988 to determine the effects of prayer on patients in the Coronary Care Unit at San Francisco General Hospital. Byrd's study found that prayed-for patients were five times less likely to require antibiotics and three times less likely to develop pulmonary edema than non-prayed-for patients. None of the prayed-for patients required endotracheal intubation, whereas twelve of the non-prayed-for patients required this procedure. In 1999, researchers from the Mid America Heart Institute at Saint Luke's Hospital in Kansas City, Missouri, conducted a more scientifically valid version of the 1988 Byrd study to determine whether remote intercessory prayer for 990 hospitalized coronary care unit patients would reduce overall adverse effects. In this replication of Byrd's study, the overall CCU course scores were significantly lower than those of the non-prayed-for patients.

In 1998, Elisabeth Targ and her collaborators at San Francisco's California Pacific Medical Center published the results of their randomized, double-blind study. They set out to determine the effects of distant healing on people suffering from advanced AIDS, controlling for variation in severity and prognosis of different AIDS-related illnesses, utilizing the Boston Health Study (BHS) Opportunistic Disease Score to measure the degree of AIDS-defining and secondary AIDS-related diseases. The distant-healing practitioners in this study came from wide backgrounds and beliefs, and the prayer treatments continued for six months. During this period, the distant-healing group required significantly fewer outpatient doctor visits, fewer hospitalizations, and fewer days of hospitalization. The group had fewer new AIDS-defining diseases and a lower illness severity level as defined by the BHS scale.

In a modest but important way, these and other scientific studies validate the importance of the spiritual dimension in human life.

Since the soul and psyche had been reclaimed by psychology and God was again in vogue, even in academic circles, in the mid-1980s I felt ready to reenter the field. I eventually earned a doctorate in psychology and became a licensed mental health professional.

PSYCHOLOGY AND KABBALAH: THE SPIRITUAL REVOLUTION

Remarkably, the paradigm shift in Judaism took place at almost the same time. Kabbalah, the Jewish mystic tradition, began to enter the Jewish religious mainstream. More and more books on Kabbalah were published, while lectures and workshops on the subject attracted large audiences. The much-publicized statements of Hollywood icons about the spiritual fulfillment they had experienced through their study of the Kabbalah were part of, and probably accelerated, this trend.

It was clear to me that the ancient truths of the Kabbalah were the bridge I had been seeking between psychology and the quest for spiritual meaning. In fact, as I mentioned earlier, the first steps across that bridge had already been taken by psychiatrist Brian Weiss, who had no knowledge of Kabbalah at the time. Dr. Weiss was founding chairman of the Department of Psychiatry at the Mount Sinai Medical Center, in Miami, Florida. His scientific research had not prepared him for his accidental clinical "discovery" of reincarnation, which I described in the preface. However, despite the recovery of his patient following her past-life regression, Weiss was not yet fully convinced. He suspected that her prior life experience might have been a false memory, but he was nevertheless open to testing the efficacy of past-life regression techniques on other patients with recalcitrant problems.

In many cases, the results were therapeutically impressive—but there was more. Some regressed patients disclosed confidential information about Dr. Weiss's family that they claimed to have received during their altered states of consciousness. There was no way anybody outside his immediate family could have had access to this information. Dr. Weiss was now certain of the existence of conscious life beyond the grave. But, suspecting that his discovery of reincarnation would be scorned by his more skeptical colleagues in the scientific community, he hesitated to publish his findings about the therapeutic effectiveness of past-life regression. However, he did mention his work to some psychiatrists at a national meeting, and he was surprised to learn that he had not been alone in his discovery. But these colleagues, too, were afraid of ridicule and had not published their findings. At this point, Dr. Weiss decided that so useful a therapeutic tool should not be withheld from the general public. The result was his best-selling volume *Many Lives, Many Masters* and several other books about the successful outcomes of past-life regression therapy.

Past-life therapy is not the only link between psychology and the Kabbalah. The Kabbalah provides a coherent and systematic account of the nature and destiny of the human soul. Jung has been rightly hailed as the most spiritually oriented of the depth psychologists. His description of the collective unconscious and the archetypes revolutionized modern analytical psychiatry. But these ideas were not new. They can be found in the sacred literature of the Kabbalah. Psychiatrist Roberto Assagioli has also been recognized as a psychospiritual innovator. Freud had based his theory of human behavior on the instinctual activities of the unconscious. Assagioli suggested that the superconscious was as important as the unconscious in directing human behavior. Freud had identified the self with the ego. Assagioli distinguished between this "Lower Self" and the transcendent "Higher Self" that each of us has. But like

Jung, Assagioli had been predated by many centuries by the writings of the masters of the Kabbalah in this respect also.

You will soon learn about the structure and nature of the human soul, and discover that the transcendent elements of our soul are the source of infinite wisdom and guidance. You will also learn how to access your higher self. You will see that the implications of these kabbalistic teachings for the nature of human consciousness are breathtaking. But there is even more that the Kabbalah can contribute to your quest for healing, growth, and the discovery of your personal calling—much, much more. The Kabbalah offers a detailed description of our spiritual DNA. It also describes how human unhappiness can always be traced to negative influences and behaviors on our spiritual DNA. When our soul structures are thrown out of balance, we begin to suffer the painful effects of dysfunctional ways of thinking, feeling, and relating. Later in the book, I shall tell the stories of some people to whom this has happened. I'm sure that you will see yourself in many of those stories.

The best news of all is that the Kabbalah is not merely descriptive, but also prescriptive. It not only describes how and why things go wrong in our spiritual genome,* but also offers effective interventions for restoring balance and achieving healing. The stories in this book all contain detailed therapeutic strategies based on both psychology and Kabbalah, pinpointing the source of the problem and the method of transformative healing. These ideas have been clinically tested, both in my office and in my three-day workshops.

---

* Strictly speaking, the term *genome* relates to an organism's genetic material. It is the complete genetic information that is passed to an individual organism by its parents, especially the set of chromosomes and the genes they carry. The human genome is the blueprint of our DNA. In this book, I refer to the building blocks of our souls as our spiritual genome. These spiritual building blocks account for the ways in which we think, feel, and interact with others.

2

KABBALAH: THE SECRET TORAH

———◄◆►———

THE MEANING OF TORAH

Most people think the **Torah** is a book, or, more precisely, the Five Books of Moses, the beginning of the Hebrew Scriptures. This is both right and wrong. The Five Books of Moses (Genesis, Exodus, Leviticus, Numbers, and Deuteronomy) are the written record of God's revelation to Moses on Mount Sinai. Jewish tradition calls that record the Written Torah. Obviously, the Written Torah is a book, but it is not the whole Torah. It is only the tip of the iceberg.

The Hebrew word *torah* means "teaching." This teaching includes the record of revelation but contains infinitely more than the narratives, laws, and moral instruction in the Five Books of Moses. The Five Books of Moses are of vital importance in themselves, but they are also the basis of a vast, dynamic body of sacred teachings that are derived from the text of the Written Torah. Indeed, even the laws contained in the Five Books of Moses are largely incomprehensible as stated in the written text. Let me give you an example. Most Jewish homes can be identified by a small rectangular box or tube on the right-hand doorpost of the main entryway. The case contains a parchment scroll with Hebrew script. It is called a **mezuzah.** Jews affix a *mezuzah* to their doorposts in compliance with a scriptural command: "And you shall write them on the doorposts of your house and on your gates" (Deut. 6:9; 11:20).

This verse does not tell us to which words "them" refers. It does not define what "doorpost" or "gate" is. It does not clarify which part of the doorpost requires the inscription. It does not inform us how many doorposts of the house require compliance with this law, and whether there are any rooms to which this command does not apply. The text doesn't tell us whether the "words" (whatever they are) should be written (or painted) directly on the doorposts, or whether, as is our practice, the two passages of the Torah that contain this command should be written on parchment in a special way, by a learned scribe, and then placed in a container and fixed to the doorpost. So how do we know, just by looking at the Written Torah, how to fulfill this command?

Let me give you a second, even more dramatic example of the problem. We know that the children of Israel offered daily sacrifices during their sojourn in the wilderness and until the destruction of the Temple in Jerusalem in 70 C.E. The written text of the Torah makes the obligation to bring sacrifices clear. It tells us also that "you shall slaughter of your herd and of your flock, which the Lord has given you as I have commanded you" (Deut. 13:21). Since the slaughtering of animals was a daily occurrence, we would have expected detailed instructions on humane slaughter. But the Torah does not tell us anything about the training and skills required by ritual slaughterers. It does not detail the type of knife to be used or the part of the animal's throat to be cut to produce instant loss of consciousness. Yet it says, "You shall slaughter as I have commanded you." No matter where in the Written Torah you turn to, you'll find no such command. How did the Israelites in the desert know what to do? How do the producers and consumers of kosher meat products nowadays know what kosher slaughtering involves? Precisely where did God detail for us the method and requirements of kosher slaughtering? The only way the children of Israel could have known how to slaughter animals in accordance with God's command is if there were an oral explanation of the command that was revealed simultaneously with the Written Torah. Without an oral explanation, there is no way they could have offered sacrifices soon after the revelation at Sinai. Indeed, there is not a single command in the Five Books of Moses that could have been performed without an oral interpretation that was as old as the written record.

The ancient sages declared, "Moses *kibbel* (received) Torah at Sinai and transmitted [what he had received] to Joshua. Joshua transmitted it to the Elders. The Elders transmitted it to the Prophets. The Prophets transmitted it to the Men of the Great Assembly" (*Avot* 1:10).* Now, since the Written Torah was taught by Moses to the entire population, the Torah that was transmitted to the individuals and groups mentioned in *Avot* must have been its ancient oral interpretation. Together, the Written Torah *(Torah she-bichtav)* and the Oral Torah *(Torah she-be'al peh)* make up the sacred "teaching" that the Jewish people call the Torah.

Although both the written text of the Five Books of Moses and its oral explanation comprise Torah, there are two fundamental differences between them. First, the Written Torah is static. Its words were, so to speak, etched in stone. It is unchanging, and, according

---

* There are two versions of the Talmud, the Babylonian and the Jerusalem. The Babylonian Talmud is more extensive and far more widely studied and used. Both versions are elaborations of an earlier work, the Mishnah, which was divided into tractates, chapters, and paragraphs *(mishnayot)*. *Avot* is a tractate of the Mishnah, and the citation is Chapter 1, Mishnah 10.

to Jewish tradition, unchangeable. In contrast, the Oral Torah is dynamic. The spiritual masters of each generation contribute their own interpretations, building upon and expanding the oral interpretation that Moses received at Sinai.

Second, the Written Torah is what it is. The text can be taken at face value and can be analyzed like any other great literary work. In contrast, the Oral Torah is multilayered, and each layer deepens our understanding of the text of the Written Torah. The Kabbalah is the deepest layer of the Oral Torah, the most profound interpretation of God's revelation. To understand where Kabbalah fits into the scheme of the Oral Torah, we must briefly examine the four levels of Torah.

THE FOUR LEVELS OF TORAH

The "teaching" that we call Torah is accessible to us on four different levels. Our sages differentiated them by using a mnemonic. They referred to the four levels of Torah as **PaRDeS** (paradise). The capital letters of this word are the initial letters of each level. The word *Pardes* itself indicates that the way to full self-realization and spiritual fulfillment is by mastering the Torah at every level.

THE FIRST LEVEL: *PESHAT*

The surface level of Torah is ***peshat*** (the simple meaning). This level is readily accessible to anybody familiar with its language, nuances, and commentaries, and can also be understood in translation. I remember my son Avi's first week in Jewish day school in New York. He came home each day excited by his introduction to the Torah. His first-grade class had begun to study the story of Creation in the first two chapters of Genesis, the very beginning of the Written Torah. At the end of the week, he had his first homework assignment. He had to tell the story of the Creation in his own words.

"Daddy," he said. "I'm sure you understand how God made the world. Will you help me with my homework?"

"Avi," I said, "to tell you the truth, I don't understand the Creation story very well."

My six-year-old was incredulous. "What do you mean?" he protested. "You're a rabbi, and you don't even know what the first chapter of the Torah means!"

I looked at him tenderly. "It's very complicated," I said. "Many great rabbis and religiously oriented scientists have spent years trying to figure out what the Torah is telling us in its first chapter. Hundreds of books have been written on the subject. Let me show you some of them."

I took him to my study and pointed to a row of commentaries on Genesis. I also showed him another section of the library. "The ancient rabbis who wrote these books were all trying to understand what the words you have been asked to explain really mean."

He looked perplexed. "What's the big problem anyway?" he asked. "The story is very simple. At first there was nothing. Then God turned it into something. We know exactly what he did every day in the first week of the world. We also know how Adam and Eve were made. So why don't you and the rabbis get it and tell the story just the way I'm going to do—without your help?"

I envied his innocence, but he did have a point. Even a six-year-old can read the *peshat* on his own level. That is the grandeur of the Bible. But I wondered if he would ever ask me just how you can make something out of nothing, how long each day of that first week was, how the story fits with the theory of evolution, what the creation of Adam and Eve tells us about all male-female relationships, what the forbidden fruit symbolizes, or why the serpent personifies the intrusion of evil and death into the world. The commentators who deal with these and myriad related questions are, like my Avi, also trying to understand the *peshat* of the text.

THE SECOND LEVEL: *REMEZ*

The Hebrew word **remez** means "hint." Here the deeper truths of the Torah are hinted at in codes embedded in the words and letters of the Written Torah. Those who know how to decode the written text discover things that are quite astounding.

One code is based on the numerical value of the words. Each Hebrew letter is also a number. *Aleph,* the first letter of the alphabet, is both a letter and also the number 1. *Bet,* the second letter, is not only the Hebrew letter *b* but also the number 2, and so on. Every word, therefore, has its numerical equivalent. If you add up the numerical value of each letter, you will get the numerical value of the whole word. This numerical coding of the text of the Written Torah is called **gematria.**

Let me give you two examples of the *gematria* code. One appears in an ancient rabbinical source. The other involves me personally. Genesis 14:14 refers to 318 men. The sages explain that this was a coded reference to one person, Eliezer, the servant of Abraham, because the numerical value of the Hebrew word *Eliezer* is 318.

My name is Abner. The numerical value of my name is 353. The phrase *ve-hay berachah* ("and you will be a blessing"; Gen. 12:2) has the same numerical value. One of my colleagues once pointed out that my name contains my mission. Everything I do in life must be a source of blessing to others. It is no coincidence, therefore, that the Hebrew word *Avner* (Abner) means "father of light." When my parents named me Abner, they must have wished that I would spread light and blessing to others. Shakespeare asked,

"What's in a name?" According to the *gematria* code, the answer is "A great deal."

Another code is known as **atbash**, in which the last letter of the Hebrew alphabet is substituted for the first, the second last for the second, and so on. This code occurs in Scripture. Jeremiah (25:26 and 51:41) refers to *Bavel* (Babylon) as *Sheshach,* its *atbash* equivalent. Dan Brown's best-selling novel *The Da Vinci Code* actually uses this example to explain the *atbash* code.

Let me share a striking example of another code with you. This code forms new words by combining the initial letters of several words, either in the order they are given by the Bible, or in reverse order. Rabbi Elijah of Vilna, the Vilna Gaon (Genius; 1720–1797), was one of the preeminent masters of the entire sacred literature of Judaism. To this day, he remains revered as a biblical commentator, talmudic authority, and towering expositor of Jewish law. His reputation as the premodern master of the Kabbalah has made him a household name among devotees of the Jewish mystical tradition. The Vilna Gaon wrote that the verse "Bow down to the Lord in the beauty of holiness" (Ps. 29:2; 96:9) conceals a secret message about the holiest, most beautiful type of worship. Its Hebrew words are *Hishtachavu la-Shem Be-hadrat Kodesh,* with the four initial letters *HLBK.* In reverse, these are the consonants of the word *Kabbalah.* According to the Vilna Gaon, therefore, immersion in Kabbalah is the most beautiful and holy worship of God.

Although there are additional codes that explain the Torah on the *remez* level, the examples I've given are enough to demonstrate that there is far more to the words of the Written Torah than meets the eye.

Some people claim that future events are encoded in the Torah, and the currently popular Torah codes that are taught in Jewish outreach seminars attempt to demonstrate that the Torah predicted such events as the rise of Hitler and the Holocaust.

THE THIRD LEVEL: *DERASH*

The third level is called **derash.** The word *derash* means "investigation" or "seeking out." This level of interpretation requires us to imagine the Written Torah as the surface of a mine containing precious metals or stones. Just as the miner digs beneath the surface in order to discover its hidden wealth, the interpreter of the Torah is required to dig deep to recover its concealed treasures. Just as the miner needs special training and equipment, the Torah explorer requires schooling in rabbinic logic and finely honed interpretive tools. This process of "mining" is known as **midrash,** a word that derives from *derash.* Using these and other methods, learned rabbis are able to uncover hidden teachings and apply them to new situations. Contemporary authorities, for instance, can guide us on what the Torah has to say about cloning, therapeutic abortion, tissue transplants, and so on. Obviously, there are no explicit references to these procedures in the Torah or clear ethical guidelines. However, they can be accessed with *derash.*

Just think about the implications of this. Every situation that ever was and that ever will be can be illuminated by the Torah's wisdom. There is no area of life on which the teachings of the Torah cannot be brought to bear. Ben Bag Bag, a first-century sage, was correct when he said, "Study the Torah again and again, for everything is in it" (*Avot* 5:26).

Derash has an additional meaning. It is also the method used by the rabbis to explore the moral lessons of the Torah. In this sense, it was the basis of ancient sermons on the verses of the Written Torah that aimed at inspiring, admonishing, comforting, and directing the Jewish people.

THE FOURTH LEVEL: *SOD*

The Hebrew word *sod* means "secret." This is the esoteric interpretation of the Torah. *Sod* is the soul of Torah. It penetrates and illuminates the profoundest truths about God, the creation of the universe, the nature of man, the existence of evil, and the purpose of human life.

The questions I raised in relation to understanding what Genesis says about the Creation can most satisfactorily be answered on the level of *sod*. On this level, biblical figures are not perceived as mere historical personalities. They are also archetypes who play a major role in the unfolding of the Divine Will in the cosmos. Adam and Eve, for example, are archetypes of the entire human species. Their sin is a metaphor for the human condition. They symbolize the dangers and opportunities of exercising free will. They personify fall and redemption, destruction and repair. In this way, the *sod* level of biblical interpretation transforms simple narratives into complex metaphors and symbols. Seen in this light, the story of the Egyptian bondage and liberation is not just a historical narrative of exile and redemption. It also reflects the experience of every human being. We all oscillate between feelings of alienation and distress on the one hand, and joy and validation on the other. All of us experience failure and success. Indeed, according to the Kabbalah, even the Divine Presence goes into exile and needs redeeming.

The Kabbalah is the *sod* level of Torah. It is, therefore, as integral a part of the Torah as Jewish law, lore, and customs—an inseparable part of the Oral Torah. The word *Kabbalah* derives from the Hebrew root *KBL*. Thus, it was part of what Moses received *(kibbel)* at Sinai, and what successive spiritual masters of the Jewish people received from their teachers. Kabbalah is the ancient, secret core of the Oral Torah.

FROM ORAL TRADITION TO WRITTEN TEXT

One of the fundamental differences between the Written and the Oral Torah is the requirement that the latter remain an unwritten, developing interpretation. Anything that is written down tends to become fixed. For this reason, the sages declared, "You are not permitted to express in written form things that were transmitted orally" (*B. T.* [Babylonian Talmud] *Gittin* 60b).* But we know that the oral tradition was written down and that commentary on these teachings makes up the great books of Jewish sacred literature: the **Mishnah,** the **Talmud,** the various collections of Midrash, and the Codes of Jewish Law. Why was the unwritten tradition transformed into written texts?

The pluses of an oral tradition are outweighed by one huge minus. A strictly oral tradition resides in the heads of its teachers. If you kill the teachers, what they know is gone forever. The enemies of Judaism believed they could destroy the religion by burning its sacred books. They made this mistake many times in our history, but as long as there were teachers who could transmit the contents of the books and their deeper levels of meaning, Judaism was safe.

The Romans finally figured out our weakness, and systematically slaughtered the teachers of Torah. This policy of extermination came to a head during the Hadrianic persecutions (about 132–135 C.E.). It was at this time that a decision was reluctantly made to commit at least some *derash* to writing in what came to be called the Mishnah and Midrash Halakhah.

Rabbi Akiva (50–135 C.E.) was the greatest sage of that period. His stamp is visible in the great bulk of the Talmud, as well as in

* The Babylonian Talmud (B.T.) is referenced by tractate name (*Gittin* in this case) and page number and side (page 60, side *b* in this case).

one of the earliest major literary works in the expanding library that now makes up the Kabbalah, **Sefer Yetzirah** *(The Book of Formation)*. *Sefer Yetzirah* is one of the most obscure of the kabbalistic texts, and is probably the earliest written record of the Jewish mystic tradition.

The crisis of that same period motivated the writing of a number of other important books on Kabbalah. Rabbi Nechunia ben Ha-Kanah and his disciple, Rabbi Yishmael ben Elisha, the high priest, transcribed the **Sefer Bahir** *(The Book of Illumination)* and **Pirkei Heichalot Rabati** *(The Greater Book of the Divine Chambers)*, which contains meditation exercises, spiritual disciplines, and directions for attaining prophecy.

At about the time of Rabbi Akiva's death, Rabbi Shimon Bar Yochai produced what was to become one of the central pillars of the kabbalistic tradition, the **Zohar** (The Book of Splendor). The Zohar is the mystical, verse-by-verse commentary on the Written Torah. Rabbi Shimon Bar Yochai had received this interpretation from his teachers, enhanced it with his own illuminating insights (there is a tradition that he was inspired by the prophet Elijah), and recorded some of those teachings in writing because he feared for his life.

The kabbalistic works of Rabbis Akiva, Nechunia ben Ha-Kanah, Yishmael ben Elisha, and Shimon Bar Yochai were seminal in the strictest sense of the word. They deliberately contained only the *seeds* of the tradition. They did not leave us completed, edited volumes. This task was left for later generations, many of whose teachers came to face the same dangers they had faced. The work of the early masters of Kabbalah was a work in progress. Many centuries after Rabbi Shimon Bar Yochai, the Zohar became the basis for two systems that dominate our understanding of Kabbalah. They were created by Rabbi Moses Cordovero (the **ReMaK;** 1522–1570) and Rabbi Isaac Luria (the Holy **Ari;** 1534–1572).

After the Spanish Inquisition in 1492, the Cordovero family settled in Safed, the center of mystical study in the Holy Land. Rabbi Moses was born there and eventually became a leading figure in its distinguished circle of kabbalists. His teaching of the Zohar was profound, systematic, and influential. It is remarkable that he accomplished so much in his short life. Later I shall quote from his seminal treatise, *The Palm Tree of Deborah,* and show how effective his strategies are for psychospiritual healing.

Rabbi Isaac Luria enjoyed an even briefer life span. His cognomen, the Holy Ari, which means "the sacred lion," derives from the initial letters of the phrase *Elohi Rabbi Yitzchak,* "the divine Rabbi Yitzchak." The Ari was probably born in Jerusalem, but grew up and was introduced to the esoteric teachings of Judaism in Egypt. After he, too, settled in Safed, he came to be regarded as the most important interpreter of the secret Torah. His teachings were recorded by his disciple, Rabbi Chayim Vital, in *Etz ha-Chayim (The Tree of Life).* This work became the basis of Lurianic Kabbalah, and has continued to inspire the most important expositors of the Zohar through the centuries. The Ari, particularly, is responsible for the formulation of the *sod* level of Torah on which this book is based.

THE WELL-KEPT SECRET

The Kabbalah was not initially meant for popular study. It was the tradition of a small rabbinic elite who had mastered the previous three levels of Torah.

You may be wondering how the contents of so many books could be kept secret. Surely their publication itself meant that the Kabbalah was generally available. The answer is that the style of the books, and their language, makes self-study exceedingly difficult.

The classical books of the Kabbalah often conceal more than they reveal. Without the guidance of an expert teacher, the Kabbalah remains hidden.

The Mishnah, edited in about the year 200, is the earliest authoritative compilation of Jewish law. It places strict limitations on the transmission of the secret part of the Torah. "The secret teachings about Creation *(Ma'asei Bereishit)* may not be expounded to two students at the same time. *Ma'asei Merkavah* (the secret of the vision of the Chariot seen by Ezekiel) may not even be taught one on one" *(Chagigah* 2:1).

The sages had forbidden public dissemination of the Kabbalah, and made their point by relating the experiences of four great sages who had ventured into this secret domain.

THE STORY OF THE FOUR RABBIS

"There were four who entered PaRDeS (paradise), Ben Azzai, Ben Zoma, **Acher** [Rabbi Elisha ben Abuyah] and Rabbi Akiva . . . Ben Azzai glanced and passed away . . . Ben Zoma glanced and lost his mind . . . *Acher* glanced and destroyed the young trees [i.e., lost his faith]. Rabbi Akiva [alone] emerged whole" *(B. T. Chagigah* 14b).

All four rabbis were great talmudic masters, outstanding authorities on the Written Torah and the *remez* and *derash* levels of the Oral Torah. Their encounter with the mystical level of *sod,* however, caused great trauma to all but Rabbi Akiva, the greatest of the four. Ben Azzai was so enraptured by his connection with God that he did not want to return to his body, but chose, instead, to die. Ben Zoma could not cope with the flashes of intuition that challenged his rationally ordered mind. Rabbi Elisha ben Abuyah lost patience with the ritual practices that had limited his life. He felt that he no longer required this traditional Jewish way of attaining spiritual fulfillment, because the glory he had experienced in PaRDeS made everything else seem trivial and insignificant. Rabbi Akiva alone was able to fully integrate the rational and mystical aspects of his personality. He recognized that the rituals themselves were divinely revealed springboards to the sublime, and that union with the Divine could be attained in everyday practice as well as in states of altered consciousness.

The tale of the four rabbis explains the great reluctance of our sages to popularize the teachings of the Kabbalah. Exploration of the sublime does have its risks, the most obvious of which is the loss of groundedness. Having tasted the sweetness of a powerful personal encounter with God, some people find everyday life frustrating and unbearable, and like Ben Azzai, yearn for death and everlasting bliss.

Schizophrenia is the ultimate loss of groundedness. Sometimes, initiation into the world of Kabbalah can reinforce and aggravate a preexisting psychotic condition. The following story is about a patient whose undirected meditation practices and explorations of the Kabbalah led him into psychiatric crisis. Clearly, Ben Zoma was not alone in the divine madness he experienced as he entered PaRDeS.

MANFRED'S STORY

Manfred Harris was referred to me by the rabbi of his synagogue because of his bizarre behavior during services. His face would contort into an almost convulsive pattern. When asked what was happening to him, he told his rabbi that he was clearing blockages in the pathway between his head and his heart. He agreed to meet with me only because I was both a licensed mental health professional and a teacher of Kabbalah.

I discovered that Manfred had had a successful career prior to his psychiatric crisis. While his condition was being managed with medication, he had joined a kabbalistically oriented community. There, he had been introduced to the unusual practice of scanning the pages of the Zohar for spiritual inspiration. He became convinced that he needed neither medication nor any other psychological treatment, and that he was the reincarnation of Adam and the key to the salvation of the human race. His strange behaviors and extravagant claims were ultimately unacceptable to the other members of the group, and he was expelled, eventually finding a spiritual home in the congregation of the rabbi who had referred him to me.

It soon became clear to me that Manfred's grandiose and delusional thinking, as well as his behaviors, had been unintentionally validated by his exposure to some kabbalistic teachings. It did not matter to him that he could not understand a single word of the pages of the Zohar he scanned. His fingers moving across the lines, he reported that God was in personal communication with him. When I suggested that what he was experiencing had nothing to do with Kabbalah but were symptoms of his psychosis, he terminated his therapy, claiming that I appreciated neither his special gifts nor the real essence of Kabbalah. I fault those who introduced him to Kabbalah for not realizing that Manfred was ill and that his illness might be aggravated by what they were teaching him.

The association of psychosis with mystical exploration is but one of the dangers of undirected study of the Kabbalah. Rabbi Elisha ben Abuyah's rejection of the norms of Jewish practice following his mystical journey illustrates a further danger. Most mystical writers tend to be antinomian; that is to say, they are against religious laws. Mystics in all but the Jewish tradition have shown little patience with religious laws, rituals, and restrictions, and have felt that the soaring of their souls have made such practices irrelevant. Indeed, those practices were often experienced by them as impediments to their spiritual paths.

The great modern expert on Kabbalah, Professor Gershom G. Scholem of the Hebrew University in Jerusalem, was accurate in his comment that Jewish mysticism differed from other forms of mysticism precisely in the significance it gave to ritual practice. One could not be an authentic Jewish mystic, he wrote, without being a fully observant Jew. The centrality of the observance of the *mitzvot* (religious commands) is attested to in every classic work in the kabbalistic library. *Mitzvot* are not impediments to spiritual growth, but, on the contrary, when they are performed with proper intention, they are its engine.

I think that the masters were reluctant to reveal the secrets of the Kabbalah for another important reason. There are three types of Kabbalah: theoretical, meditative, and practical. Rabbi Aryeh Kaplan, a prolific modern teacher of Kabbalah, writes that "the theoretical Kabbalah essentially gives us a description of the spiritual realm. Meditative Kabbalah tells us how to get into this inner space. Very often the theoretical Kabbalah is an important guide once you are in there . . . it gives you landmarks . . . in other words [it lets you know] which world you are in, whether on the side of good or of evil. The third type is practical, or magical, Kabbalah."

This quotation from Rabbi Kaplan's introduction to Kabbalah, *Innerspace,* highlights two dangers of undisciplined Kabbalah practice. The first is the peril of entering unfamiliar, sometimes dangerous, territory. The second relates to the magical power contained in some kabbalistic teachings, practices, and incantations. In the wrong hands, this power can be destructive.

SECRET NO LONGER

If all this is true, you must be wondering, why have I written this book? And why has Kabbalah suddenly gone public? The great philosopher Georg Wilhelm Friedrich Hegel (1770–1831) introduced to Western thought the concept of the zeitgeist, the spirit of an age. For many years I did not understand this concept. It was too abstract and vague. But I am now convinced that there is such a thing as the spirit of an age. Why else should my very young grandchildren be at home with computers, while I remain cybernetically challenged? My grandchildren and their generation have been affected by the contemporary zeitgeist. I believe that the sudden universal interest in Kabbalah is also part of the spirit of our age.

Indeed, Rabbi Elijah, the Vilna Gaon, predicted that the growth of scientific knowledge would be matched by a yearning for mystical enlightenment. According to one of his students, Rabbi Hillel Rivlin of Shklov, he implied that ours would be the generation both of unprecedented advances in science and interest in the mystical experience.

The Zohar (1:117a)* also taught that the public revelation of the secret Torah would be conditional upon the exponential growth of all scientific knowledge: "In the year 600 of the sixth millennium [of the Hebrew calendar] (1842 C.E.), the gates of celestial wisdom will be opened together with the channels of human wisdom. This will be at the beginning of the gradual process of messianic revelation."

---

* All scholarly editions of the Zohar make use of its standard pagination. The first number (1, in this case) is the volume, the second (117, in this case) is the page, and the letter (*a*, in this case) is the side.

The suggested date coincides more or less with the beginning of the scientific revolution. This revolution has been exponential. Think of things that are commonplace today. We communicate instantaneously by e-mail. How long ago was it that the World Wide Web was used only by the scientific elite? We matter-of-factly process documents on laptop computers. Do you recall how recently computers with less power would require a mainframe housed in a significantly sized room? Do you remember when space exploration was the domain of science fiction? How long ago was it that no one knew what DNA was? Could my high school biology teachers have grasped the concept of the human genome? When I was a six-year-old, *wireless* was another word for *radio*. Nowadays, we have cell phones, which are wireless miniature computers. A dozen years or so ago, long-playing records were replaced by CDs. Currently, DVDs are replacing videos. There has been more scientific progress in the past century than in all the millennia that preceded it.

The Gaon of Vilna died about forty years before the Zohar's predicted date of the beginning of the messianic process. He considered the teaching of the Kabbalah to be an essential precursor to the redemption, claiming that the redemption of truth goes hand in hand with the redemption of humanity. Therefore, he regarded the dissemination of the secret Torah as his personal mission. He even went so far as to say that anybody who studied the Torah on its simple, *peshat* level could be correct only if the *peshat* agreed with its mystical interpretation. In other words, he held that all authentic study of the Torah required knowledge of the Kabbalah.

Thus, I do not need to apologize for helping bring Kabbalah into the mainstream more than 200 years after the Gaon's passing and 160 years after the Zohar's predicted date for the public dissemination of Kabbalah.

PSYCHOLOGY AND KABBALAH

The scope of Kabbalah is vast. It covers theology, philosophy, cosmology, revelation, parallel universes, human nature, and much more. And these topics are all interconnected. On the other hand, psychology, as it is commonly understood, is far more restricted in its scope. It has been defined as the disciplined study of human behavior and experience. Theology, cosmology, revelation, and the notion of parallel universes are not relevant to psychology when it is defined in this way. But if the definition is broadened to include consideration of the human spiritual genome, the nature, structure, and history of the human soul, and the impact of spiritual energies, both dark and light, upon functional and dysfunctional ways of thinking, feeling, relating, and being in the world, then many of the kabbalistic topics I have mentioned do become psychologically relevant—especially since they are all interconnected. Therefore, we have to learn about the most important doctrines of the Kabbalah, its teachings about spiritual energies, the spiritual genome, and the human soul to fully appreciate what it has to tell us about human nature, thought processes, emotions, relationships, and fulfilling and self-defeating behavior. The wisdom of the Kabbalah permits us to see these things in an entirely new way.

3

THE ESSENCE OF KABBALAH

—◈—

GOD IS BEING

The main teaching of the Kabbalah is that God is Being. This statement is deceptively simple. It is also unutterably complex. Two stories from the Torah will help explain its meaning.

The first is Moses' initial encounter with God. He was tending his flock in the desert of Midian, when suddenly, he noticed a remarkable phenomenon. He saw a bush that "burned with fire, but the bush was not consumed" (Exod. 3:2). Then God, speaking from the mysterious bush, asked Moses to go to Pharaoh and the children of Israel and tell them that he would liberate the slaves from their bondage in Egypt.

Since neither he nor that generation of Hebrews had previously encountered God directly, Moses said, "Behold, when I come to the children of Israel and say to them, 'The God of your fathers has sent me to you,' and they say to me, 'What is his name?' what shall I say to them?" (Exod. 3:13).

God responded to this question somewhat enigmatically. Tell them, he said to Moses, "***Ehyeh** Asher Ehyeh shelachani*. I AM THAT I AM has sent me" (Exod. 3:14). The Hebrew verb *ehyeh* shares a common root, HVH, with the noun ***havayah*** (being). When *ehyeh* and *havayah* refer to God, they are capitalized. God is Being. In other instances, they are written in lowercase, as in "human being." So when God identified himself to Moses for the first time, he simply referred to himself as Being, with a capital *B*. What did God wish to teach Moses by identifying himself in this way?

The Torah says, "The Lord God fashioned Adam from the dust of the earth" (Gen. 2:7). It describes how that clay figure became a living human being: "And he breathed into his nostrils the breath of life, and Adam became a living soul" (Gen. 2:7).

The Zohar invokes a powerful image to explain this. "One who exhales," it declares, "exhales some of one['s life force]." The reader is immediately reminded of mouth-to-mouth resuscitation. A victim of a drowning accident is pulled from the water, unable to breathe, apparently lifeless. Using the "kiss of life," the rescuer literally breathes his or her own breath into the victim's lungs, transferring life force into the victim. According to the Zohar, what the Torah is describing in the story of the creation of Adam is God's kiss of life. The first human being would have remained a clod of earth were it not for the fact that conscious Being was poured directly into it.

Havayah gave the gift of being to Adam when it poured itself into him. By the same token, had *Havayah* been removed from Adam, he would have reverted to his lifeless condition. The message of Adam's creation, then, is that anything that has Being—not only human beings, not only an Adam, but anything that exists in the infinite reaches of the cosmos—exists only because it contains *Havayah,* Godness—even the earth from which Adam was fashioned. So what God did for Adam was to give conscious human being to the clay figure by animating it with his own Being.

The stories of the burning bush and of the creation of Adam raise a fundamental question: How can something as insignificant as a desert thornbush or as finite as a single human being contain infinite Being within itself? The answer is the key to the central message of the Kabbalah.

STEPPING DOWN DIVINE ENERGY

The process that enables infinite Being to reside in finite beings can be clarified with a commonplace illustration. The electricity of many great cities is generated by nuclear reactors. If your home is part of such a grid, you're usually not conscious of the source of the electrical energy that is so readily available to you. You flick a switch, and the reading lamp on your desk goes on, providing you with illumination appropriate for your needs. The light in the bulb is usually quite limited. The energy it is using is an infinitesimal proportion of the nuclear power at the source of the grid. That power is enormous.

When the nuclear reactor in Chernobyl failed in 1986, and some of the energy leaked out, so great was its power that people within a radius of hundreds of miles were sickened. Many died and others developed leukemia and other forms of cancer. The workers who were sent to repair the damage risked their lives. The first nuclear explosions over Hiroshima and Nagasaki at the end of World War II had taught the world a terrible lesson about nuclear power. The energy released by those small bombs was so great that things in their direct path were not merely pulverized, but were annihilated, because nothing can coexist with raw energy of such indescribable power.

Nevertheless, properly harnessed and controlled, the energy at the core of a nuclear reactor can become available for such benign uses as the illumination of your desk by your table lamp. This process is a function of a system of filters and transformers. You realize you are benefiting from the illumination, but you also know that the light bears almost no resemblance to the energy at the core of the nuclear reactor. Now imagine that all the world's nuclear energy was combined in a single reactor. The light and energy at its core would be almost beyond human comprehension. If direct exposure to a relatively low-grade nuclear explosion brings annihilation, what would exposure to the power of a super nuclear reactor do? Now imagine that we were exposed to the direct energy flow of the sun. Its annihilating effects would far exceed those of the super reactor. Let your imagination take you even further. Imagine that the energy of every star in our solar system and in every other constellation were combined and directed unfiltered at the earth. There would be no earth. All earthly existence would instantly disappear without a trace.

The energy and light that emanates from God is beyond anything we can imagine. It is infinite in every way. Coexistence with that energy is inconceivable. And yet, like the illumination in the humble desk lamp, the divine energy came to reside in the desert thornbush, in Adam and all his descendants, and, indeed, in everything that has being. Just as the energy at the core of the nuclear reactor is stepped down, filtered, and transformed, the divine energy can reside in and energize finite creatures.

I have used the metaphors of light and energy interchangeably. Light is a visible form of energy. It is thus an effective way of describing the flow of the energy of *Havayah*. Light is filtered differently by different materials. It is not perceptively affected by a transparent filter, but not all transparent materials are equally transparent. In some, a careful observer can notice the distortion. In others, the distortion is almost imperceptible, and there seems to be no barrier interrupting the flow.

Translucent materials, on the other hand, do impede the flow.

They permit the light to pass through them, but to a far lesser degree than transparent materials. A frosted window affects the light differently than does a clear pane of glass. The dark film that covers the glass facades of modern office buildings is also translucent, but less so than frosted glass. The effect of translucent materials is to reduce the power of the light and to transform its appearance. Opaque materials block the passage of the light. They appear to be impervious to its rays, yet they, too, are affected by light. When the light shines on them, they become visible.

The Kabbalah provides us with an elaborate description of God's filters, transformers, and step-down mechanisms. The parallel universes and the Ten *Sefirot,* the divine energy system about which you will soon learn, perform this function.

THE PARALLEL UNIVERSES

Just as pure light is invisible, the light of Absolute Being is invisible. It is also unimaginable. The Kabbalah calls the source of ineffable, pure Being the ***Ayn Sof*** (limitlessness). ***Ayin*** is the Hebrew term for "nothing." With a capital *A,* as it were, *Ayin* means "No-thingness." Absolute Being, therefore, is infinite No-thingness. We cannot comprehend infinite No-thingness, because no thing (nothing) in our experience can define it. Absolute Being manifests itself as it emanates from utter incomprehensibility through dimensions or universes that are increasingly less subtle and, therefore, more comprehensible. The existence of these parallel universes is fundamental to kabbalistic cosmology.

If I had written about the existence of parallel universes just two decades ago, I would have been accused of a fanciful flight of imagination. Amazingly, the most up-to-date scientific theory now supports the notion of various realms of existence. Also, this theory is no longer confined to scientific publications. The national press has shared scientists' excitement about the existence of multiple dimensions with millions of readers. For example, K. C. Cole's "Column One" in the *Los Angeles Times* of Saturday, May 17, 2003, carried the title "A New Slice on Physics: Theory Alters Physics' Big Picture." The article tells us that in the last few years, a mathematically rigorous cosmological model has refashioned the way physicists think about everything from subatomic particles to the big bang.

> The universe we see, according to this scenario, is stuck on a thin membrane of space-time embedded in a much larger cosmos. And our membrane may be only one of many, all of which may warp, wiggle, connect and collide with one another in as many as ten dimensions. Physicists call this new frontier "the brane world." . . . Stephen Hawking of the University of Cambridge, among others, envisions brane worlds bubbling up out of the void, giving rise to whole new universes. He ends his latest book, *The Universe in a Nutshell,* with a call to explore this "brane new world." (Cole, pp. A1, A22)

One may wonder how reputable scientists have accepted the existence of multiple universes that nobody has ever seen or experienced. Harvard University physicist Lisa Randall and her Johns Hopkins University collaborator, physicist Raman Sundrum, answer this perplexing question:

> The reason: We can't see anything outside our brane, because light can't escape or enter it. We can't hear anything outside, because sound travels through matter, and matter is stuck to our brane. We can't use radioactivity to sense what's beyond, or even break through with nuclear

bombs, because nuclear forces are also firmly nailed to our brane. There could be a big blue elephant sitting not a millimeter away in another dimension, but we wouldn't know it's there because everything we use to "see" is stuck to our brane. (Cole, p. A22)

The Kabbalah does not limit itself to the ten dimensions alluded to in Cole's article and by the string theorists. It maintains that it is impossible to enumerate all these parallel universes and for the most part elaborates on the nature of five of them.

The first of these five universes is conceptually almost indistinguishable from pure Being. It is so much a part of Being that it is simply called *Ayin,* No-thingness.

The second, the universe of **Atzilut** (Emanation), is another descending unfolding of Being from *Ayn Sof.* The word *atzilut* is related to the Hebrew word *eitzel* (next to). The makeup of the beings in this realm is extraordinarily subtle because they are so close to primal Being. They lack almost all form and substance. But they are not pure Being, and their function is to filter the light. They do distort the light, but almost imperceptibly. The realm of *Atzilut* is where the Divine Will to emanate beings from Being manifests, and is a universe beyond human experience.

The third is known as the realm of **Beriyah** (Creation), and is the world of souls. The world of *Beriyah* is further removed from the Source than the world of *Atzilut.* Therefore, the beings in this realm are less subtle than those in the realm of *Atzilut,* for they are composed of energy filtered through the layers of that realm. Their less subtle nature presents a greater barrier to the flow of light. The realm of *Beriyah* is still transparent, but much less so than *Atzilut.* The transformation of the light is far more apparent here, although it is still imperceptible to human eyes.

Because the divine light continues to pass through more filters and transformers in the realm of *Beriyah,* the beings in that realm range from the highest to lowest degree of *Beriyah* subtlety. A wide range in the subtlety of beings exists in each of the five cosmic realms.

By the time the light reaches the realm of **Yetzirah** (Formation), the fourth of the parallel universes, its energy has been stepped down considerably, and it is barely transparent. Its beings reflect the decreasing subtlety and power of the divine energy, and can be perceived by humans with developed inner vision— prophets, seers, and advanced meditators. *Yetzirah* beings are the angels of which the Bible speaks, and masters whose souls have progressed far beyond the earthly realm.

The Kabbalah calls the lowest realm **Asiyah** (Action). This is the spiritual root of our material universe. When the light of Being reaches this level, the stepped-down process is complete. Humankind occupies the highest spiritual position in the realm of *Asiyah.* We are uniquely capable of creative activity, but are not all on the same spiritual level. Some people are so evolved that the light of Being appears to shine through them. These are the great spiritual masters who have completed their earthly evolution after many incarnations and have come back from the higher realms to lead and teach others. Moses is a striking example. When he descends from Mount Sinai, his face shines so brightly that he needs a mask to protect others from its effulgence.

> And it was when Moses came down from Mount Sinai with the two tablets of testimony in Moses' hand, when he came down from the mountain, that Moses did not know that the skin of his face shone while he spoke unto him. And Aaron and all the children of Israel saw Moses;

and behold, the skin of his face was radiant. And they
were afraid to approach him . . . he placed a veil on his
face, but when Moses came before the Lord to speak with
him, he removed the veil until he came out . . . and the
children of Israel saw the face of Moses, that the skin of
Moses' face shone; and Moses again put the veil on his
face until he went in to speak with him. (Exod. 34:29, 30,
34–35)

His connection to Being is so direct that the Torah says of him that
he discourses directly with God, and not through a glass darkly,
like the other prophets.

And he said, "Please listen to my words. If there were a
prophet among you, I the Lord would make myself
known unto him in a vision, I would speak to him in a
dream. Not so my servant Moses . . . mouth to mouth do
I speak to him, manifestly and not in a dim reflection. He
looks directly at the likeness of God." (Num. 12:6–8)

There are other very gifted human beings who are far less evolved
than Moses. Nevertheless, they have attained a very high level.
They are not as transparent to the divine energy as Moses was, but
the light still shines through them. These are the other prophets,
saints, seers, and great spiritual teachers, often pictured with halos.
All human beings have some degree of translucence, because the
human soul is a spark of the Divine. Some have developed their
spiritual potential to the extent that their inner light shines forth.
Their halos can easily be seen by clairvoyants, and have even been
captured on film. The halos of those who are less spiritually
evolved are dimmer and less brightly colored. And there are some
people who have blocked their light so much that it can hardly

illuminate their own lives, let alone the lives of others. Most of us belong to this category. We are unconscious of the power of Being in our inner core. We are not aware of the divine energy within us that can be tapped and released for healing, growth, and self-realization.

Animals, plants, and minerals also depend upon the divine light, and if the divine light were not to shine upon them, they would not exist. Because everything reflects godness, everything is potentially sacred.

CREATION FROM NOTHING

As you have seen, the parallel universes are the stages in which the ineffable *Ayin* becomes more and more palpable. They reflect the emanation of *Havayah* (Being) from pure No-thingness to some-thingness. The Hebrew term for "thingness" is **yesh.** The process of emanation is therefore described as the emergence of **yesh mi-Ayin** (something from No-thingness).

Because *Havayah* clothes itself in the five universes, the Kabbalah associates each with a letter of the tetragrammaton, the unpronounceable Hebrew four-letter name of *Havayah (yud, hay, vav, hay)*. The first universe, *Ayin,* is incomprehensible. Therefore, it is indicated by the tip of the smallest letter of the Hebrew alphabet, *yud.* The realm of *Atzilut* is associated with the rest of the letter *yud. Beriyah* is associated with the first letter *hay* of the tetragrammaton. *Yetzirah* reflects the letter *vav,* and the realm of *Asiyah* is the embodiment of the second *hay,* which is the last letter of this holy name. The Hebrew word for "universe" is *olam.* The word *olam* is also associated with the word *ne'elam* (hidden, concealed). The paradox of creation is that the divine light of these five realms is concealed within their manifestations.

MEDITATION EXERCISES:
AN INTRODUCTORY COMMENT

Four guided meditations are included in this book. Each follows a presentation of largely abstract concepts, transforming them into a lived spiritual experience. You will learn a great deal about the benefits of regular meditation later in the book. For now, I hope you will be assured that the discipline and time required for regular meditation is worth the effort. You can maximize the benefits of the printed meditations by recording them and listening to the tapes, seated comfortably with your eyes closed. Alternatively, you may choose to purchase a CD of the meditations that I have recorded. You will hear my voice over music in which theta meditation pulses are embedded to help entrain your brain waves to this kind of spiritual experience. Please see page 287 for details about the CD.

MEDITATION ON BEING

1. Remove your shoes and loosen any tight clothing.
2. Sit comfortably on a chair, with your back straight and your hands, palms up, on your lap. Gently close your eyes.
3. Be aware of your body. Feel your weight.
4. Inhale through your nose, filling your diaphragm with air. Hold your breath as you count to five. Exhale through your nose, feeling the tension leave your body on your exhalation. Repeat this cycle five times.
5. Remain conscious of your breathing and listen to the sound as it goes in and out.
6. Imagine you are sitting in a waterfall of gentle, blue light. See it surrounding you, enveloping you, caressing you, healing you, and comforting you. Stay with this image.
7. Imagine that the light is passing through the crown of your

head, filling your head with its healing glow. Let the light in your head wash away the tensions in your mind, relax the tension in your eyelids, cheeks, mouth, and jaw. The light of Being is soothing and relaxing, relaxing and soothing.

8. Let the light pass into your neck, relaxing its muscles, easing away its tensions. Your eyes, cheeks, mouth, jaw, and neck are more and more deeply relaxed.

9. Let the light continue on its passage through your body, relaxing the tight muscles in your shoulders and upper back. Feel the tension ease.

10. Let the light pass into your upper arms, relaxing your triceps, biceps, and all the complex muscle groups of your upper arms.

11. Let the light pass through your elbows, relaxing your forearms. Feel the tension in the muscles of your forearms ease. Allow the light to pass through your wrists into your hands. Be aware of how the muscles in your hands and fingers relax and the tension leaves them.

12. Let the light pass through your fingers, rejoining the soft blue waterfall of light that continues to envelop you. That light both surrounds you and flows through your head, neck, shoulders, arms, hands, and fingers in an unending cycle of swirling, healing light.

13. Let the healing light now pass from your head and neck into your chest, caressing and relaxing your heart, cleansing and relaxing your lungs, washing the tension from all the organs of your upper torso.

14. Let the light pass from your torso to your hips. Let it pass from there into your thighs. Let the muscles relax and experience the tension leaving your thighs.

15. Let the light pass from your thighs through your knees and into your calves. Feel the muscle groups of your calves relax and the tension drain away.

16. Let the light pass through your ankles into your feet, washing the tension from your soles and relaxing your toes.

17. Let the light pass from your feet into the ground. There is

light everywhere. It surrounds you and encompasses you. It fills you and relaxes you. You are one with the light.

18. Picture yourself in a meadow at the top of a hill. You can smell roses and honeysuckle. You can hear the songs of the birds. You feel the sun warming your face.

19. You begin to walk through the grass, aware of the rustling sounds of the breeze through the grass, sensitive to how the grass feels underfoot. You feel alive and well.

20. You come to the end of the meadow and begin to walk down the path between the trees. The leaves rustle gently in the breeze.

21. The farther down the hill you go, the more deeply relaxed you become. Relaxed and at ease. At ease and relaxed. Each step brings you into deeper relaxation. Your eyelids are heavy.

22. Below you, at the bottom of the hill, you see a clearing. You know that you are nearly at your destination. With each step you take, you relax more and more deeply. Three more steps. Go deeper into relaxation. Two more steps. Go deeper still. One more step. You are very deeply relaxed and at ease.

23. The clearing is a place of almost unearthly beauty. The grass is lush and green. It is surrounded by tall trees casting their shadows and their patterns of light. You notice a long, flat rock by a stream. You sit down on the rock and rest.

24. You look up and notice a leaf detach itself from a tall tree. You watch it gently turning this way and that, that way and this, as it descends ever so slowly on the breeze. As the leaf descends, you descend with it, even more deeply into relaxation. You watch the leaf turn this way and that, that way and this, every second relaxing more deeply. The leaf comes to rest on the water, and you watch as it continues its journey, and gradually disappears from view, having brought you into the deepest state of relaxation you have ever experienced.

25. As you sit on your rock, you think of someone you love deeply—a spouse, a parent, a child. Let that love fill your heart. Stay with that love. Enjoy its energy.

26. Now let the love energy move upward into your head, filling your mind with loving thoughts. Stay with that love. Stay with those gentle feelings and thoughts.

27. Allow the feeling of love to rise above your head, three feet, six feet, or even sixty-seven feet. Feel the love in your heart, in your head, and high above you.

28. Now feel a new love energy descending to meet you, bathing you in golden light.

29. Picture the loving feelings in your heart as golden light. Let that light fill your entire chest. Let it rise and fill your head. Let it rise above your head three feet, six feet, or even sixty-seven feet, joining itself to the golden light that bathes you.

30. You are light. You are love. You are divine energy. You are part of nature. You are connected to Being. You are Being.

31. Remain in this blessed state as long as you want to. Feel your oneness with the Infinite. Feel your oneness with Being and light.

32. When you are ready, you may gently retrace your steps up the hill, becoming more and more awake with each step. When you are at the top of your hill, you can open your eyes, refreshed by your meditation, able to recall every step of your journey to tranquillity and wholeness.

4

THE HUMAN SOUL

---◄◊►---

THE NATURE OF THE SOUL

When I first lectured on the nature of the soul, I asked members of the audience to tell me what they thought it was. The suggestions fell into two categories. One person said, "The soul is a little spiritual person inside of us. It's the spiritual clone of our bodies. That spiritual person is the invisible engine that drives us." Most people agreed with her, although their own precise descriptions varied. The views of the other group were summed up by someone who said, "The soul is indefinable. It's simply the divine spark in all of us."

According to the Kabbalah, the soul is not a spiritual clone of the body. Nor is the soul merely a spark of the Divine. The soul is far more complex than any member of the audience could have guessed.

Just recall the Torah's description of the creation of Adam, which provides us with a vivid image of the infusion of Being into his clay form. The Being within him was his soul, "a part of God above." This is, in fact, the way classical Jewish literature defines soul.

Unfortunately, this description of Adam's creation may be a little misleading. There is a significant difference between God's breathing the breath of life into Adam, making him into "a living soul," and the resuscitation of a drowning victim. Once the victim is able to breathe again, no further intervention by the resuscitator is required, and apart from an emotional connection that may have taken place, no essential connection remains.

The creation of Adam was radically different. If the connection between Adam's being and Being had been severed, Adam would have reverted to his lifeless state. Indeed, even the vessel of clay would eventually have disintegrated. Adam's vitality depended upon his continued connection with the divine energy that vitalized him.

In his pioneering study *Rabbinic Psychology,* Rabbi W. Hirsch cites a Torah source for this definition of the moment of death: "And it was, as her soul departed, because she died, that she named him *Ben-oni* (the son of my affliction). But his father called him Benjamin (the son of my right hand). And Rachel died and was buried . . ." (Gen. 35:18–19). Once the soul has departed, the human being is dead.

In the jungles of my native Africa, vultures are known to circle over mortally injured people. The moment death comes, the vultures swoop down. Somehow, they seem to sense the passing of the soul. At that moment, the remains become a carcass instead of a living body.

Jewish practice requires someone to remain with the body of the deceased until burial, lest the body be attacked by mice. On its face, this requirement is puzzling, since mice are afraid of humans. Why, then, should a human body need to be protected from them? It appears that mice, too, know the difference between a living human being, however frail, and a dead body. In the natural world, the separation of soul from body is intuited as the signal of transition from life to death.

The Bible uses poetic imagery to describe death as a break in the connection between the human being with the Source of Being. Ecclesiastes, the Preacher, urges us to remember our Creator while we are young, before the onset of physical frailty and weakness. He describes the gradual loss of vision, the trembling of the arms, the weakening of the spine, and the loss of teeth. This leads him to his beautiful description of death itself: "When the silver cord is severed and the golden bowl is broken . . . then shall the dust return to the earth as it was; and the spirit shall return to God who gave it" (Eccles. 12:6–7). The image of the silver cord is found in the sacred literature of both East and West. It is sometimes invoked to explain our dream journeys when we sleep. The cord that attaches us to our body has sufficient slack to permit us to journey through the astral plane, but it ensures that our soul remains connected to our body when we awaken from our slumbers. The silver cord is a marvelous metaphor for the soul. It evokes the umbilical connection between the mother and her developing fetus. The human soul is the umbilicus that connects our being to Being, the Source of our sustenance and vitality, and death occurs when it is severed.

THE STRUCTURE OF THE HUMAN SOUL

The Kabbalah describes the human soul as having five elements that parallel the unfolding of the Divine through the five universes. The act of cosmic creation, as I described it, is the process of stepping down the energy of God until it becomes accessible and manifest. Because the human soul is divine, it also undergoes this process. It exists in two dimensions, which psychologists call personal and transpersonal. Most people think of the soul only as it functions within the body. This is its personal dimension. However, there are elements of the soul that are not incarnated. They exist before we are born and survive our physical demise. Because they are disembodied, they are called transpersonal. Two of the soul's five elements are embedded and active in our bodies, two are transpersonal, and one is partly personal and partly transpersonal.

THE SOUL'S TRANSPERSONAL ELEMENTS

Jung described the way people tap into what he called the collective unconscious when they dream, and demonstrated how it affects our emotional states and contributes to our healing and growth. The fact that so many of his patients experienced this makes the concept of a dimension beyond the body more believable to us. In chapter 1, you learned that at roughly the same time as Jung was writing about the collective unconscious, a great Italian psychiatrist, Roberto Assagioli, posited the existence of "super consciousness," which he called the "Higher Self." Assagioli's clinical findings led him to distinguish between the activities of the embodied elements of the soul (the "[Lower] Self") and the disembodied Higher Self. Transpersonal theorist Ken Wilber has described the transpersonal elements of the soul and their impact on our lives in his various books, particularly *A Brief History of Everything*. However, none of these experts has described the soul's transpersonal elements in as much detail as the Kabbalah.

The first three stages of the unfolding of our souls from their infinite Source in Being are transpersonal. On its highest level, the soul is indistinguishable from the *Ayin,* the divine No-thingness, and so the Kabbalah calls it **Yechidah** (Unification), derived from the Hebrew root YChD, "togetherness." Because this element of the soul is united with the *Ayin,* it is unknowable.

The Kabbalah calls the soul's next element, which is associated with the realm of *Atzilut* (Emanation), **Chayah** (Living Essence).

Like the other forces in the realm of *Atzilut,* this element is still undifferentiated and is part of the collective soul of all humankind. Divine energy unfolds through the realm of *Atzilut,* becoming less transparent. The collective also unfolds into more differentiated collective souls, such as the collective soul of Israel. But, even as it unfolds and differentiates, the soul remains attached to its Source in the *Ayin.*

Soul individuation occurs in the realm of *Beriyah* (Creation). It is here that myriad individual souls assume their personal characteristics, still remaining attached to their Source through the unfolding collective souls. The individual human soul is called the **Neshamah,** and its primary function is cognitive. It is active in two dimensions, playing a vital role in our spiritual lives both inside and outside our bodies.

The transpersonal element of the *Neshamah* is linked both to the collective human memory and to memories of the segments of humanity. Thus, for example, the *Neshamah* of a Jew is connected to the soul and memory of the Jewish people and, through that, to the soul of all humanity. The Talmud (*B.T. Niddah* 30b) employs a beautiful metaphor to describe this dimension of the individual Jew's *Neshamah* prior to its physical incarnation. "A lamp is lit above his head. Through its illumination, he scans and looks from one end of the world to the other . . . and they teach him the entire Torah, as it is written, 'And he instructed me and said to me: let your heart retain my words. Keep my commandments and live (Prov. 4:4).' And it is said: 'When the counsels of God surrounded me like a tent (Job 29:4).' " In this way, the sages visualize the connection of the individual *Neshamah* to the collective levels of *Chayah* and *Yechidah,* and imagine its illumination. This out-of-body dimension of the *Neshamah* surrounds the individual, encompassing him or her with energy, light, and wisdom. The Kabbalah calls this state of the soul

Or demakifin (surrounding illumination). This light, as I pointed out in the last chapter, is sometimes visible as our halo.

Because it is connected to *Chayah* and *Yechidah,* this part of the *Neshamah* is the conduit to divine and collective human wisdom, and facilitates our intuitive and creative processes. It is also the memory bank of our experiences over previous lifetimes. I shall be discussing the kabbalistic belief that our souls are incarnated many times and that the purpose of each of these incarnations is to help us on the road to spiritual perfection. Although most of us are not conscious of our experiences in other lifetimes, our memories of those lifetimes remain embedded in our *Neshamah.* Later in this chapter, you will see how past-life experiences influence our current emotional and spiritual well-being.

Three elements of our souls are embedded in our bodies, each with its own special functions and interrelationships, and each less subtle than the preceding. They are the incarnated parts of the *Neshamah,* the **Ru'ach** and the **Nefesh.** In ascending order, the soul has five elements: *Nefesh, Ru'ach, Neshamah* (embodied and disembodied), *Chayah,* and *Yechidah,* which are known by the acronym formed by their initial letters, **NaRaNCHaY.** However, it must be emphasized that the soul does not have different parts. It is an indivisible entity that has various functions and is active in different dimensions, connecting us to our divine Source and infusing us with godness. The Kabbalah refers to the "elements" of the soul only to facilitate our understanding of its functions.

THE STRUCTURE OF THE EMBODIED SOUL

Let me return, for a moment, to the creation of Adam. His suscitation was described as God's breathing into his nostrils. This metaphor teaches us a great deal about the nature of the soul. The Hebrew word for "breath" is **neshimah.** It is almost the same word as *Neshamah,* the most subtle element of the embodied soul. The Hebrew word *Ru'ach* means "wind." God's breathing the living soul into Adam, therefore, is pictured first as a gentle breath and then as a powerful rush of air that suffuses his body. The Hebrew word *Nefesh* is associated with the verb *va-yinafash* ("and he rested" [Exod. 31:17]). It describes how the breath came to rest in Adam and transformed him from a clay humanoid figure into a living soul.

Thus, the Torah uses the metaphor of the breath to describe the process of ensoulment. Rabbi Aryeh Kaplan has compared this process to the intentions and actions of a glassblower fashioning a delicate vessel. In the beginning, the artisan's vision of the completed vessel is inseparable from his own essence. He exercises the will to translate his vision into reality. He blows into the molten glass until it is filled and shaped in accordance with his vision. Finally, the air settles and the task is completed. The stages of vision and will represent the *Yechidah* and *Chayah* elements of the soul. The implementation of the vision is represented by the introduction of the divine energy into the raw material of cells and tissue through the first gentle breath *(Neshamah)*, the increasing perfusion of rushing breath *(Ru'ach)*, and the completion of the process *(Nefesh)*. To be sure, the analogy, as always, is imperfect. The glassblower removes himself from the completed vessel. In contrast, the Creator is attached to the individual as long as he or she remains a human being.

THE FUNCTIONS OF THE *NEFESH*

The *Nefesh* is the interface between soul and body, the bridge between the worlds of spirit and matter. Its main function is our safe and healthy survival in our physical environment. Because the *Nefesh* is the element of the soul most intimately bound up with our physical functions, the Bible associates it with the blood that flows throughout our bodies.

The *Nefesh* governs such mechanisms of survival as eating, drinking, reproducing, and protecting ourselves. These aspects of physical survival require humans and animals, which also are endowed with *Nefesh,* to move around, run away, and, if necessary, to attack. In humans, the *Nefesh* is also closely involved in psychological defenses against people who wish to control us with mind games by exploiting our emotional vulnerabilities, and through unhealthy relationships. But, apart from these defenses, the functions of our *Nefesh* are largely indistinguishable from the instinctual responses of other animal species. Like other animals, we salivate when we are hungry, and if our instinct for reproduction were not restrained, we would, like animals in heat, locate any available partner with whom to couple, consensually or nonconsensually. When physically challenged, we fight, hide, freeze, or flee. So the *Nefesh* is often called *ha-Nefesh ha-behemit* (the animal soul).

The ultimate purpose of the *Nefesh* is to transform the human body into the sacred temple of the soul. It achieves this purpose if it is able to refine its instinctual impulses. Most animals do not discriminate between permitted and forbidden foods. They simply eat when they are hungry. But human beings can be discriminating. Our food discrimination runs the whole gamut. Some of us will ingest even those things that are harmful to us, simply because they provide us with immediate gratification. Some of us will confine ourselves to the ingestion of things that are healthy. Some will even avoid certain foods in obedience to the dietary laws of the Torah. Some realize that they can become gluttons on kosher food and, therefore, limit their diet not only to the permissible, but also to the necessary. Even then, they ingest their food consciously, first considering its divine source and offering blessings for the gift of sustenance. On the level of nourishment, therefore, the *Nefesh* can be either animalistic or spiritual.

Consider, for a moment, the instinct of reproduction. Our

sexual encounters may be motivated by the desire for immediate gratification. Some people are incapable of making exclusive relationship commitments or of controlling their predatory instincts. Some will even rape unwilling partners. However, most people will exercise self-control, and some will even avoid relationships with partners whom the Torah does not consider eligible, such as those whose previous relationships have not been dissolved in accordance with Torah requirements, close relatives, and members of other faith communities. Some go further and limit the occasions of sexual intimacy in accordance with the laws of family purity. Some, whose instincts are still more controlled, will impose further limitations on themselves in accordance with their own standards of personal piety. These examples demonstrate that the *Nefesh* can either refine the realm of *Asiyah* or be overwhelmed by its materiality.

THE FUNCTIONS OF THE *RU'ACH*

According to the Kabbalah, the *Ru'ach* controls our emotions. Action is always driven by emotion. Our desire to eat precedes the act of eating. Our desire for particular substances is motivated by our longing for them. Similarly, the gratification of our sexual impulses is the direct consequence of our desires. The extent to which we surrender to our animal instincts or control them is influenced by our emotions. Our ability to impose will on instinct— that is to say, to refine the activities of the *Nefesh*—is one of the main functions of the *Ru'ach,* the dimension of the human soul from which the *Nefesh* directly unfolds. Herein lie both opportunity and danger. While the *Ru'ach* can refine the *Nefesh* when it controls primitive impulses, providing opportunities for spiritual growth, the danger is that our will to resist our animalistic tendencies can be eroded by a pattern of surrender to uncontrolled gratification. When this happens, the *Nefesh* overwhelms the *Ru'ach,* transforming it and increasingly concealing its divine light.

This ancient understanding of the interrelatedness of our emotions and appetites has been validated by the success of Alcoholics Anonymous in achieving sobriety for millions of people. Its twelve-step program has become the treatment of choice for a wide variety of addictions. AA alone has more than a million active members in more than eighty-seven thousand groups in over a hundred countries. Its program has been adapted to more than a hundred other disorders besides alcoholism (Emrick, 1994).

Six of the twelve steps mention God or a Higher Power. Step twelve concludes, "Having had a spiritual awakening as a result of these Steps . . ." It is clear that the essence of the program is religious/spiritual and its successful outcome is defined as "a spiritual awakening." Carl Jung understood the role of the spiritual dimension in recovery. He wrote to Bill Wilson, the cofounder of AA, who happened to be one of his patients, "His craving for alcohol was the equivalent, on a low level, of the spiritual thirst of our being for wholeness, expressed in medieval language: 'the union with God.' " Christina Grof, an expert in the treatment of addictions, contemplating her own recovery from alcoholism, wrote in *The Thirst for Wholeness: Addiction, Attachment, and the Spiritual Path* that she "became acquainted with the 12-Step programs and discovered that they contain, in ordinary Western language, many of the elements that had attracted me to various spiritual systems" (p. 4). She added that "12-Step programs talk about the addict's experience of soul sickness . . . Addicts face spiritual bankruptcy as they reach the bottom" (p. 19).

Jung, Grof, the founders of AA, and the other organizations to which it gave rise were saying what the masters of the Kabbalah had said long ago. Our *Nefesh* can become a source of dangerous hedonistic living. In time, our appetites can control our lives if the light of divine inspiration becomes dim. However, the nature of a flame is to reach upward, and however dimly the spark glows, it yearns to grow in brightness. A soul, no matter how low it has sunk, craves spiritual fulfillment. This teaching is the strategy of most successful recovery programs. At their core is the conviction that achieving spiritual meaning can conquer the most terrible addictions.

Let me share two stories with you.

ALIZA'S STORY

Aliza was referred to me for follow-up treatment by a well-known rehabilitation center. She was the child of affluent Turkish parents and had almost always been granted every wish. As long as she was a loving daughter and caring sibling, she lived an unrestricted life. The circles in which her family moved "knew how to live." They worked hard and also partied hard. Many drank excessively, all were heavy smokers, and many used drugs recreationally.

When Aliza's family moved to the United States, they continued the same way of life. As a young adult, she began to drink heavily. Aliza's life was interrupted by the long, fatal illness of her young mother. Drinking for pleasure transformed itself into drinking as self-medication. Because drinking was acceptable in her social circle, it took her family a long time to recognize that she had become an alcoholic.

Aliza's stay at the rehab center was very effective. I decided to involve all the members of her family in her ongoing treatment, which was ancillary to her local twelve-step program. The focus of my work with Aliza and her family was a search for spiritual meaning. Together, we began to discover her calling to work as a therapist and help others in trouble. Her enrollment as a psychology major was a further step in her transformation. Aliza's days were no longer spent either at home alone or socializing with friends whose lives revolved around partying. She and her family became involved in the local religious community, and eventually, Aliza declared, "Doctor Weiss, I am amazed. I no longer need to drink."

I was not amazed. Aliza's life had become purposeful and her days meaningful. Her *Ru'ach* was no longer dominated by her *Nefesh,* which was being transformed by her powerful newfound spirituality.

JASON'S STORY

Nobody is immune to the seductive power of the *Nefesh.* Not even rabbis. I had known Jason before he decided to become a rabbi. He was a charismatic young man, whose soul seemed to be on fire. His peers were entranced when he led them in Chasidic song and worship, and his spiritual teachings were mesmerizing. As a member of his informal religious community, he was often invited to share his insights on the Torah reading, and he became the lay leader of his community. Seeing his great gifts, I encouraged him to enter the rabbinate. I felt he had a natural talent and a clear religious calling.

Jason heeded my advice and went to study in a seminary in Israel. Following his ordination, he was invited to stay on to do outreach work. He soon became the Pied Piper of his community, gradually extending his sphere of influence beyond the walls of the seminary. People came to the lectures he gave at his home, and the kabbalistic thrust of his teaching attracted a larger and larger following. Unfortunately, his charm was particularly seductive to some of his female followers. Although he was married, he had a number of affairs with women students, who were led to believe that his connection with them was primarily spiritual.

Jason's sexual appetites could not be concealed forever. Eventually, his wife left him, and he was thrown out of the seminary. He returned to the United States and moved to a community far from the centers of Jewish population. He reckoned that his past was unlikely to catch up with him in his new environment. He began to attend services at the local synagogue, soon volunteering to teach there. It was not long before he had gained a significant following of his own and was invited to set up an independent, breakaway congregation. It was also not long before he remarried. Once more, he began to connect with his female followers, claiming that his love for them was purely spiritual, and he became involved with the wife of his leading sponsor. When she discovered that she was not his "other half" but merely one of his many lovers in the community, she had a breakdown, and he was driven out of the city. Remarkably, his wife agreed to remain with him if he would seek treatment for his sexual addiction.

Jason came to see me and I accepted the responsibility for his treatment after he'd contracted with me to join a twelve-step program for sex addicts. Jason's sessions with me took the form of an in-depth reexamination of his religious commitments and spiritual ideas.

His story is a tragic example of how the *Nefesh* of a gifted person can corrupt his *Ru'ach* and even his *Neshamah*. Jason had been misled by his rationalization of his behavior. He had been unable to distinguish between lust and love; he had believed that his lust was genuine spiritual connection and, in so doing, had all but destroyed his own life and the lives of his victims.

I've described the *Ru'ach*'s control of the *Nefesh* as a major function of the soul's emotional faculty. However, emotional control alone does not provide for happiness and spiritual growth. On the contrary, too much control and defensiveness can block our experience of love, as well as our appreciation of beauty, harmony, and truth. It can account for anger, rage, and emotional anesthesia. Healthy, fulfilling relationships, benevolence, and tenderness are achieved through emotional intelligence, which is a function of the psychologically productive interface of *Ru'ach* and *Neshamah*.

THE FUNCTIONS OF THE *NESHAMAH*

The *Neshamah* facilitates our thought processes, mediating our intuitions and our analysis of insights and what we have learned from books, people, and life experience. It acts as an antenna for receiving ideas from our higher selves and our collective soul. The intuitive aspect of the *Neshamah*'s activity is captured in the talmudic passage to which I've already referred (*B.T. Niddah* 30b; see page 52). There it says that the embryo is granted access to all the truths of the Torah and the cosmos, literally seeing "from one end of the earth to the other." However, at the moment of birth, when its lips are touched by an angel, it forgets what it has learned. Here the sages were teaching us that we can access enormous reservoirs of supernal truth and the unconscious knowledge we have accumulated through many incarnations, and that wisdom is available to us by honing the antennae of our *Neshamah*. Intuition is a gift, but we are able to enhance the ways we can receive it. Whereas creative intuitions seem to pop into our minds from outside of us, the analytical work of the *Neshamah* is accomplished through the accumulation of knowledge and by critical thinking. The way the *Neshamah* mediates intuition and processes thought is a function of divine energy systems called *Sefirot*. You will learn much more about these engines of cognition in chapter 5.

In addition to the *Neshamah*'s purely theoretical function, it has a vital practical role. In 1995, psychologist Daniel Goleman introduced the innovative notion of "emotional intelligence." According to Goleman, human intelligence consists of far more than our ability to think logically and be creative. It includes other human competencies, such as self-awareness, self-discipline, persistence, and empathy. The Kabbalah discussed emotional intelligence many centuries before the publication of Goleman's work. The human competencies Goleman described are also functions of the *Neshamah,* and the bridge between thinking and feeling. This bridge is the interface between the activities of *Neshamah* and *Ru'ach.*

Ru'ach does not function in isolation. It is inseparably linked both to the *Nefesh* and the *Neshamah.* For example, we come to love people as a result of our positive thoughts about them, and we fear them only after we have negative thoughts about them. The more we think they will hurt us, the greater our urge to attack them or escape from them. There is both opportunity and danger in the interface of *Ru'ach* and *Neshamah.* In its pristine condition, while our emotional intelligence remains uneroded by our primitive passions, the *Neshamah* can transform the negative aspects of the *Ru'ach* and, as a result of this transformation, the animalistic aspects of the *Nefesh.* The danger is that our *Neshamah* can be corrupted. When we habitually surrender to primitive desires, our thought processes are gradually affected. Reason is replaced by rationalization, and self-regulation by self-justification, as the *Neshamah* begins to strategize ways of fulfilling unacceptable desires.

Our divinely ordained mission on earth is the transformation of the realm of *Asiyah* into the "kingdom of God." But we are granted free will. We are able to choose to impose uncompromised intellect on emotion and action. When we do so, the divine light within us becomes stronger and stronger and affects our material environment. As I have pointed out, it also affects the entire cosmos. We can, on the other hand, choose to blunt our intellectual sensibilities, rationalize our most primitive urges, and act on those urges. By making that choice, we have failed to accomplish our divine mission on earth.

REINCARNATION: *GILGUL NESHAMOT*

Fortunately, God, with infinite mercy, gives us many opportunities for achieving our mission. The Holy Ari devoted an entire section of the *Etz ha-Chayim* (Tree of Life) to a description of the many journeys of the individual soul. The Kabbalah calls reincarnation *gilgul neshamot.* Every lifetime provides new opportunities for spiritual progress and the correction of past mistakes. This is known as *tikkun* (repair). Every successive incarnation is a chance to rectify old wrongs and missed opportunities. However, while we accrue merit over many lifetimes, we are also capable of subverting our previous achievements.

Once we have achieved our full spiritual potential, we have no further need to be reincarnated in physical bodies. At that time, our souls continue their evolution in the invisible universes, *Yetzi-rah, Beriyah,* and *Atzilut,* coming ever closer to unification with their Source on the soul level of *Yechidah.*

There is one striking exception to this law. Highly evolved souls sometimes choose to become teachers and religious masters in order to assist others in their personal spiritual growth.

LIFE AFTER DEATH

Belief in life before birth and after death is fundamental to Judaism. The first prayer we utter in the morning after we have cleansed ourselves is our acknowledgement that "the soul you have given me is pure. You created it, formed it, and breathed it into me. You preserve it within me. You will, at some future time, take it from me. And you will restore it at some future time."

The main element of Jewish worship is called the **Amidah** (standing prayer), which is recited three times a day, and more often on Sabbaths and festivals. Its first paragraph reminds us of the divine connection with those who have gone before us. The second paragraph is called "the Mighty Acts of God." These include the ordering of the seasons, provision of sustenance, healing the sick, release of the bound, and commitment "to those who sleep in the dust." The blessing that summarizes all the mighty acts of God is significant in that it focuses on life after death: "Blessed are you, God, who gives life to the dead."

Moses Maimonides (1135–1204), the greatest of the Jewish theologians and philosophers, outlined the thirteen fundamental principles of the Jewish faith, the last of which relates to life beyond the grave. An old Jewish proverb has it that "the last is the most precious," so, obviously, Maimonides wished to emphasize the importance of belief in personal immortality by locating it at the end of his principles.

Readers who are familiar with the Hebrew Bible may be wondering why it does not deal systematically with the subject of life after death, given its doctrinal and liturgical importance. After all, the holy writings of other ancient religions and philosophies have emphasized the notion of personal immortality. The Eastern teachings about reincarnation, maya, and nirvana depend on the conviction that the soul survives physical death. The Tibetan Book of the Dead prepares the dying for what they will experience beyond the grave. The notion of life after death pervades the theologies of the ancient Fertile Crescent. Significantly, the Egyptian "bible" is actually called The Book of the Dead. Classical Greek philosophy considered personal immortality as a given. Plato, for example, reasoned that since the soul alone has clarity about the most important matters in life, its incarnation in a mortal body and its preoccupation with corporeal matters may serve only as a distraction from what is really important. Therefore, he concluded that the philosopher may justifiably look forward to death as a release from bodily limitations (*Phaedo* 67d). Gnosticism's and Judaism's daughter religions, Christianity and Islam, emphasize life after death. Christian theology focuses on reward and punishment beyond the grave, elaborating the notions of hellfire, purgatory, and heavenly recompense, and the Koran describes in great detail the rewards of the righteous in paradise.

In my opinion, the relative silence of the Hebrew Bible about the soul's survival of bodily death was a reaction to the harmful social and moral consequences of overemphasizing life after death in other religions. The Jewish experience in ancient Egypt is a good example. Egyptian priests were so preoccupied with what happens beyond the grave that they failed to correct social atrocities. This is why they could remain silent about the dehumanization, exploitation, and suffering of the Hebrew slaves and countenance a policy of the systematic murder of newborn male children. Apparently, physical suffering and social injustice did not bother Egyptian priests because they were convinced of the transience and, therefore, the relative insignificance of corporeal existence in comparison with eternal life beyond the grave.

Moses responded to the callous indifference to suffering engendered by the culture of death by forbidding Jewish priests from having any contact with the dead. For Judaism, the quality of life on earth cannot be diminished by expectations of "pie in the sky when you die." Social justice is at its very core. Its religious leaders were primarily charged with the concerns of the living. The Torah reacted to the moral paralysis that had resulted from disproportionate emphasis on personal immortality, not by denying the reality of life after death, but by emphasizing, instead, the human mission of transforming this world into the kingdom of God through the creation of institutions of justice, mercy, and charity. In the twenty-first century, people whose sense of security has been eroded by random acts of terrorism would have no difficulty in sympathizing with the Torah's reaction to a culture of death. We are outraged by the indiscriminate killing and maiming of innocents by "martyrs" anxious to earn eternal bliss by killing themselves and others to glorify God.

However, notwithstanding Judaism's uncompromising embrace of the challenges of earthly human existence, its Scriptures are not silent about our survival of physical death. Allusions to personal immortality are scattered throughout the Bible. For example, death is defined as the separation of the soul from the body (Gen. 35:18; 1 Kings 19:4; Jer. 15:9; Jon. 4:3), and is described as the return of the body "to the dust from which it comes," when "the spirit returns to God who gave it" (Eccles. 12:7). The biblical belief in continued consciousness after death is reflected in King Saul's consultation with the woman of Endor to channel the spirit of the prophet Samuel (1 Sam. 28:7–25), and the scriptural prohibition against relying on the souls of the departed for guidance (Lev. 20:6, 27; Deut. 18:11; Isa. 8:19).

Separated by many centuries from the Jewish experience of the cruelty of the Egyptian religious culture of death, the sages of the classical rabbinic period deal with the belief in life after death far more explicitly. Rabbis W. Hirsch and Elie Kaplan Spitz have published detailed accounts of this aspect of rabbinical doctrine.

The Jewish belief in life after death has, since the mid-1970s, been reinforced by the rigorous examination of the so-called near-death experience (NDE). Psychiatrist Raymond Moody noted striking similarities in the description of the experiences of many of his patients who were diagnosed as being clinically dead, but who subsequently "awoke." In all these cases, the absence of detectable signs of life such as respiration, heartbeat, and other reticular activity had been documented in their charts. Most of his NDE patients reported that they had seen themselves floating above their bodies, observed medical staff trying to revive them, and had traveled through some kind of tunnel of light to meet deceased relatives. Many described being welcomed by benevolent figures, and recalled their out-of-body experiences as blissful. They told Dr. Moody that the events of their lives had unfolded before them in a flash, and none of them wished to return to their bodies. However, they did return because they were told that their earthly tasks had not yet been fully accomplished.

The report of one participant in Moody's study is very significant since he was a Russian doctor who had been educated by the Soviets to deny both the existence of God and the soul. His surprise at his near-death experience was palpable. I have seen his interview with Moody on film and was particularly impressed by his spiritual transformation following his "revival."

The research of Australian sociologist Dr. Cherie Sutherland confirms the widespread nature of NDE. These findings have been further reinforced by the near-death experiences of young children. These reports are especially significant because small children are generally shielded from death and are not taken to funerals. Although children are not aware of the detailed narratives of adults about their near-death experiences, they report the same phenomena as adults. Their descriptions of a tunnel and other aspects of the near-death experience have been collected by pediatrician Melvin Morse in his book *Closer to the Light*. Clearly, the near-death experience is universal and throws light on the nature of death and dying.

LIFE BEFORE BIRTH

Just as research by Raymond Moody, Kenneth Ring, Melvin Morse, Cherie Sutherland, and others reinforces Jewish belief in conscious life after death, the work of psychiatrists Brian Weiss and

Adrian Finkelstein validates the ancient kabbalistic conviction that there is conscious existence between bodily incarnations.

I have already referred to the use of hypnosis in the recovery of memories of past-life experiences. However, I always hoped that I would have the opportunity of testing what others had done. My opportunity came quite unexpectedly.

EDWARD AND BETTY'S STORY

At the time this happened, I was head of the rabbinical court of Los Angeles and was blessed to have touched the lives of many remarkable people who wished to convert to Judaism. One day, I received a call from a husband and wife, neither of whom was Jewish.

When I met them, I was impressed by their sincerity. The husband, Edward, had been a well-educated, nonpracticing, and nonbelieving Christian whose secular convictions were completely unsatisfying. After much soul-searching, he abandoned his comfortable middle-class life and set out in search of the truth in a Himalayan ashram. He spent more than seven years in ascetic living and meditative practice, and, eventually, wrote a book on Eastern religions. But the spiritual emptiness that had driven him from America persisted.

He returned to the United States and met Betty, a woman who shared his deep spiritual yearning. They married, established a home in Southern California, and began to research other paths. They had read a great deal about Judaism and its mystical tradition, and joined a welcoming community, whose rabbi understood their needs and hoped that they would find fulfillment in Judaism.

The couple studied diligently, committed themselves to the practice of the divine commandments *(mitzvot)*, and the day of their formal conversion was approaching. Edward's excitement about the culmination of his spiritual search was growing. However, I sensed Betty's hesitation and decided to raise the issue directly with her. She told me she had begun to have serious misgivings about converting but did not understand why. She was happy about everything she and her husband had learned, she loved her community, and she found her rabbi inspiring.

I asked Betty to go home and talk the matter through with her husband. Perhaps Judaism was not to be her chosen path. Perhaps she had suppressed her true feelings because she did not wish to upset Edward. Betty called me a few days later and asked if she could come to see me in my professional capacity—not as a rabbi, but as a psychotherapist. I told her that since her problem was related to the conversion process, she could regard an additional meeting with me as part of that process.

As soon as she sat down in my office, Betty came straight to the point. "Rabbi," she said, "I am also a psychotherapist. Long before you spoke about my unconscious fears, I knew that I had become phobic about converting to Judaism. This really upset me because my rational mind wants nothing more than my conversion. Please help me understand my phobia."

Acting on a hunch, I asked her whether she had had any personal experience of hypnosis. She assured me that she had. I probed more deeply. "Have you ever read about past-life-regression hypnosis?" I asked. Betty nodded. "Yes, I've read *Many Lives, Many Masters.* I was so fascinated by what I read that I bought several other volumes on past-life regression."

"Great," I said. "Would you like me to do some past-life-regression hypnosis with you?"

"I'm glad you asked," she said. "It has occurred to me for some time that my conversion phobia may have something to do with an experience in a previous life."

Betty was easily hypnotizable and regression to her child-hood was quick and extremely vivid. Eventually, she remem-bered the earliest days of her life, so I asked her to go back to before she was born, to another life, in another place.

She described a small village in Poland in great detail. I asked her what language the people were speaking and she said it was Yiddish. I knew that Betty had not learned Yiddish in her current life, so I asked her if she could speak in that lan-guage, and she did. She also described her family, what they were wearing, the appearance of their house, and so on.

Finally, she relived the pogrom. The Nazi butchers had entered the town. There was shooting and shouting and scream-ing everywhere. She saw her parents and brothers and sisters cut down. Her own death was not as swift. She described how a huge man had lifted her up by one hand and hurled her, head first, at the wall of the house, scarcely waiting for her to lose consciousness before shooting her dead.

Betty's terror of becoming Jewish now made sense: The memory of her experience had lingered in the recesses of her unconscious. I instructed her to retain that memory in her conscious mind, and, still under hypnosis, to see the little girl who had been murdered standing next to the mature woman she now was. I asked her whether she could see that her life in Poland was over, and that her soul was now in a different body, living in a place where being Jewish was a privilege rather than a curse. She answered that she could.

When Betty awoke from her hypnotic trance, her relief was palpable. I was not surprised when she told me that she was no longer afraid of converting and that she was eagerly looking forward to the experience.

The problem with most past-life memories, including Betty's, is that the events patients recall during hypnosis cannot be easily corroborated. Fortunately, some cases have been verified. The experience of a patient of Los Angeles hypnotherapist Dr. Bruce Goldberg is a great example of verifiable memories and later became the subject of his book *The Search for Grace*. A woman had come to him because her husband was abusive. Her submissive response to his violent outbursts had empowered him to maintain his behavior. Contemporary psychologists would label her codependent. She recalled under hypnosis that in a previous lifetime in a small town in upstate New York, she had been murdered by her husband, and that she was now married to the reincarnated soul of her murderer. Goldberg realized that she needed to be empowered to end the cycle of continuing abuse by finally leaving her husband this time around.

After the resolution of his patient's problem, Dr. Goldberg set about verifying her memories. She had described the details of the murder vividly, and had given Goldberg her name and that of her husband in that previous life. She had also described the town, supplying street names and mentioning other local landmarks. Those details were no longer public knowledge. In fact, the murder had not been widely reported beyond that small town. The town no longer looked the way she described it, and even street names had changed.

Goldberg's search was successful. He found the marriage certificate in the official records and reports of the murder in both the newspaper and police archives. He used old maps of the town to satisfy himself that the places she had described under hypnosis had, in fact, existed.

It seemed to Goldberg that the drama of this particular dysfunctional marriage was the stuff of which interesting books and good movies are made. He contacted CBS, which also saw the potential of this documented case of murder and reincarnation. CBS sent its own researchers to upstate New York. They tracked down descendants of the murdered woman and her husband to discover whether they had ever had any contact with Goldberg's patient. None of them had, and none of the current residents of the town was familiar with the facts of the murder. After many days of careful investigation, the researchers assured the network that it could go ahead with the project without fear of embarrassment. The resulting CBS television movie was a dramatic validation of recovered memories from previous incarnations.

Hypnotherapy had reinforced what devotees of the Kabbalah had long known about the redemptive function of reincarnation. Both Betty and Grace had been given a fresh opportunity for *tikkun*. Betty completed her interrupted spiritual journey, and Grace learned how to take care of herself.

5

THE SPIRITUAL GENOME:
HOW WE THINK

---◄◆►---

THE TEN *SEFIROT*

Earlier, I wrote about the unfolding of the universes, both invisible and visible, and the transpersonal and personal dimensions of the human soul from *Ayn Sof.* The Kabbalah reveals God's blueprint for this process, and describes how all beings emanate from Being. Both the blueprint and the creative process are contained in the primordial Tree of Life, which consists of the ten most powerful refractors of divine energy in the cosmos. These vessels of light and energy are known as the Ten *Sefirot* and are the building blocks of everything that exists (see Figures 1, 2, and 3).

The Hebrew word *sefirah*—the singular form of *sefirot*—is related to the word *sapir,* which means "sapphire," "brilliance," or "luminary." The beauty of an exquisitely cut precious stone comes from its many facets, each revealing different colors and color nuances of the spectrum. Understood in this way, the *Sefirot* are prisms that break down the invisible divine light and manifest its different characteristics.

Sefirah is also related to the word *sefer* (book), because the doctrine of the *Sefirot* tells the secret story of the process of creation. In addition, the word *sefirah* derives from the same root as the word

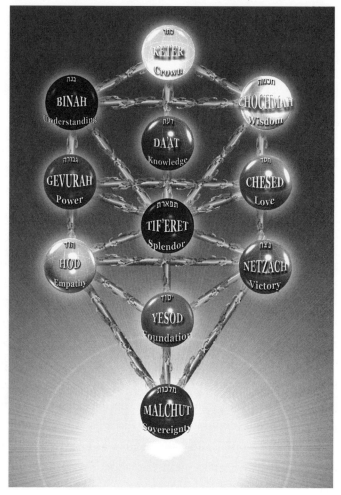

1. The Tree of Life: Linear Representation

sefar (boundary). This is because the Ten *Sefirot* form the blueprint for the cosmos and every created thing, inanimate, vegetable, animate, human, and angelic. Finally, the word *sefirah* shares the root letters of *safar* (cipher or number). This is because the Ten *Sefirot* explain the numbered stages of Creation. The Tree of Life, literally, permits us to "decipher" the secret code of Creation.

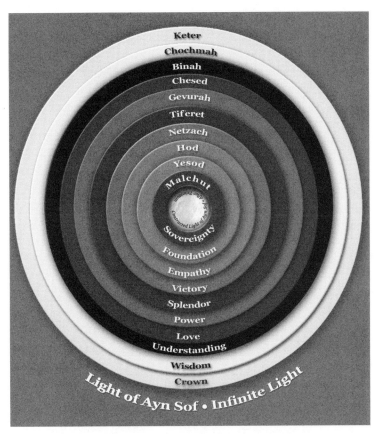

2. *The* Sefirot: *Circular Representation*

The DNA molecule is a good model for further clarifying what I mean. Most of us are familiar with the theory of DNA. The DNA molecule determines the genetic structure of all physical organisms. If it were stretched out, our DNA double helix would be about eight feet long and would contain approximately 3 billion bits of information that are the blueprint for and the building blocks of our physical selves.

The Ten *Sefirot* are the spiritual equivalent of DNA. The spiritual DNA is not a mere eight feet in length. It does not contain a

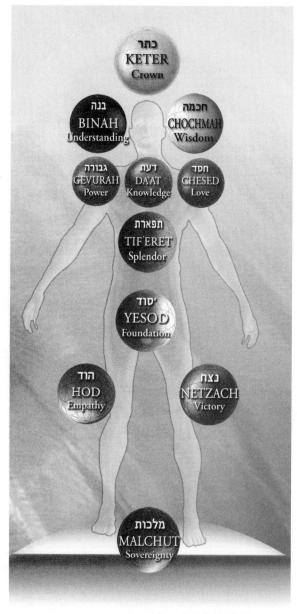

3. The Human Energy Centers: The Microcosm

mere 3 billion bits of information. The endless permutations of the Ten *Sefirot* account for the being of everything that exists, and knowledge of the spiritual DNA is as vital to our understanding of reality as knowledge of the physical DNA molecule is for understanding the genetic structure of living creatures. As Rabbi Yechiel Barlev puts it in *Song of the Soul*, "From the structure of the *Sefirot*, we can understand the structure of reality at any level" (p. 81). Thus, the structure of the human being, in all its facets—the physical, the psychological, and the spiritual—is contained in the Ten *Sefirot*, which are in perfect balance and harmony when we are born, notwithstanding our prior life experiences.

The first *Sefirah* triad is made up of *Keter, Chochmah,* and *Binah.* Kabbalistic literature refers to this triad by the acronym **KoCHaB.** The capital letters of the acronym are the initial letters of the first three *Sefirot.* These *Sefirot* are the spiritual blueprint for all cognitive processes.

KETER: THE FIRST *SEFIRAH*

The Hebrew word *keter* means "crown." **Keter** is the interface between Infinite Being and Creation. It partakes of the quality of infinite No-thingness. But it is impossible for us to speak intelligently about infinite No-thingness. Therefore, it is also impossible for us to speak meaningfully about *Keter.* This is why the Kabbalah often refers to *Keter* as *Ayin* (concealed No-thingness). All we can say about *Keter* is that it is the *Sefirah* of will. It is the first emanation of the Divine Will. Will precedes thinking, planning, and action. For God, willing was the first stage of creation.

Willing is also the initial stage of every human endeavor. My building a house presupposes my initial desire to build it, my

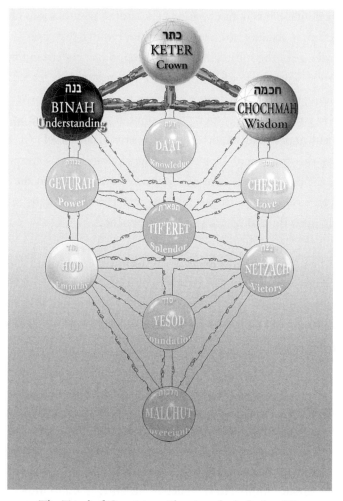

4. *The Triad of Cognition, Showing the* Sefirah *of* Keter

thinking about the project, my building plan, and my execution of
that plan. But no one can be certain why I acted upon them, only
that I decided to do so. My action, by itself, does not reveal all
aspects of my will. It follows that if even human will is concealed,
the Divine Will is certainly also concealed. That is why kabbalists
rarely say much about *Keter*. They do not go beyond the notion

that the Divine Will to create must have emerged from the divine essence before God contemplated Creation.

What all kabbalists do say about *Keter* is that the word's meaning—"crown"—tells us something important about its essence. Just as a king's crown rests upon his head and is separate from him, so *Keter,* as it were, is separate from the other nine *Sefirot.*

At first glance, it may seem that *Keter* has no direct bearing on human behavior, but this is not the case. An example from Jewish law will show you what I mean. A religious divorce requires mutual consent. The law assumes that the overwhelming majority of people are decent. However, the sad reality is that some people are scoundrels, who refuse to consent to a rabbinic court's order to execute a divorce, out of spite or a desire for financial gain. These dishonorable people use Jewish law as leverage. They blackmail their spouses by offering them their freedom only if they relinquish what the secular courts have granted them, or if they pay huge sums of money.

The talmudic sages were well aware of human nastiness, and ruled that a recalcitrant spouse can be coerced into saying, "I wish to grant the divorce." But how can such a statement reflect a person's real willingness to cooperate? The sages resolved this conundrum by distinguishing between the higher will and lower will. One's lower will may be motivated by prudence, convenience, or greed. One's higher will, a reflection of *Keter,* reflects one's better nature and uncompromised spiritual state. Therefore, when a recalcitrant spouse declares, "I wish to grant the divorce," it is really his higher will, his better nature, that is speaking. Two stories put human faces on this distinction.

JOAN AND PETER'S STORY

My connection with Joan and Peter was unusual. They belonged to the local Reform temple, and I had never met them. One day, I received a call from their rabbi asking if he could discuss a moral problem with me. Joan and Peter had had a stormy marriage, which had ended in a civil divorce twelve months earlier. Most Reform rabbis do not require a religious divorce in addition to a civil dissolution. In fact, none of his predecessors at the temple had urged their congregants to comply with Orthodox and Conservative religious law in this respect. My colleague's problem was twofold. On the one hand, Peter's family enjoyed great prestige and had real financial clout in his congregation. They supported Peter's refusal to go through with an "unnecessary" religious divorce procedure. On the other hand, Joan had grown up in a more observant home and had told the rabbi that she could not remarry without receiving a religious divorce. Joan hoped to remarry one day and felt trapped. The rabbi was torn between the ethical imperative of helping Joan to gain full personal freedom and taking on powerful elements in his congregation who could claim support of Reform tradition for their position.

The rabbi asked me what kind of leverage Joan had, hinting that her ex-husband might cooperate if he received a substantial sum of money from her family. I replied that this kind of blackmail was intolerable and, instead, put him in touch with a Jewish women's rights organization. The leaders of this organization made numerous attempts to persuade Peter to release Joan. At first, he heard them out, but soon became abusive, slamming the phone down on them and failing to return their calls. When they attempted to visit him at his home, he threatened them with a restraining order.

The organization concluded that something more than moral suasion was required. If Peter's callousness was motivated by financial considerations, it was likely that financial considerations would motivate his compliance. They began to picket Peter's business. Their placards urged people not to do business with a person who was torturing his ex-wife. Peter attempted to rid himself of the nuisance. But when he got a restraining order, the demonstrators merely crossed the street, and more volunteers joined the protest every day. Some followed his delivery vans and continued their demonstration outside the homes of his customers. Someone must have told Peter of my widely known association with the women's rights organization. I began to receive nasty phone calls from him, demanding to know how a rabbi could condone such ugly pressure. I gently reminded him that his consent to a religious divorce in the presence of three qualified people would resolve the problem. He cursed me and hung up. Four days later, his rabbi called, conveying Peter's consent, and that day Joan received her freedom.

Peter's refusal to permit Joan to get on with her life was the result of his pragmatic lower will. I believe that his ultimate cooperation was not merely a surrender to pressure. A finer part, the higher will, which mirrored his *Keter,* unconsciously brought him into compliance. Indeed, his rabbi subsequently told me that after Peter had dealt with his rage, he confessed that contrary to his expectations, he was feeling better about himself and that in freeing Joan, he had freed himself to get on with his own life, unencumbered by bitterness.

YVETTE AND SEYMOUR'S STORY

Yvette was the child of a Moroccan Jewish family that had emigrated to France, and Seymour was from Brooklyn, New York. They met at a party in Paris and had a brief courtship. They were sure that their common Zionist passion was more important than the cultural divide that separated them. Each had already decided to emigrate to Israel, and so, immediately after their wedding, they moved to Tel Aviv and had a son and daughter. But life in the new Jewish state proved to be extremely stressful, and their shared Zionism was not sufficient to keep them together. Seymour dismissed Yvette's Israeli family as North African primitives. He was especially resentful of the fact that their transplantation to Israel had been more successful than his, and that Yvette had turned to them for help when he lost his job. His rage and frustration grew with each additional month of unemployment. His love for Israel was replaced with anger, and he often said that if he had stayed in the United States, he would not have lost his self-respect.

Initially, his anger was expressed verbally, but eventually he became physically abusive, blaming Yvette and her family for frustrating his desire to leave Israel with the children. He refused to go for counseling. Yvette and the children moved in with her family to avoid further abuse, and she applied for a divorce in the local rabbinical court. Her husband shrewdly told the judges that her reason for wanting out of the marriage was because she was less Orthodox than he was. He suggested that if she were to live in a religious environment for six months, she would see the error of her ways. Although his claim was untrue, the judges believed him, and she and the children had to move to an exclusively Orthodox village. At the appointed time, Yvette returned to the rabbinical court, bringing witnesses both from her past and from where she was now living to attest to her undiminished piety. The panel summoned Seymour, demanding that he initiate the divorce proceedings. When he failed to respond to the summons, the court imposed a number of sanctions on him, which included an order restraining him from traveling abroad until he complied with the execution of the divorce. But before the order could take effect, he left Israel on his American passport.

Seymour deliberately kept his whereabouts a secret, and not even his parents knew where he was. But during the course of the next decade, he would send Yvette a birthday card from a different part of the world, claiming that he still loved her and could not bear to let her go. Eventually, their son came to the United States to attend college, and somehow tracked his father down and tricked him into a meeting. He threatened his father with serious consequences if he did not immediately accompany him to a local rabbinical court to execute the divorce. To the end, Seymour insisted that he had withheld the divorce out of genuine love for Yvette. The rabbinical court dismissed this plea and had him sign a power of attorney permitting the process to commence.

I have no doubt that Seymour believed he was holding on to Yvette because he loved her and that eventually she would see the error of her ways and return to him. I am convinced that these were the promptings of his lower will serving his self-interest. There must also have been another part of him, his higher will, that prompted him to accompany his son to the court. A person of his ingenuity, who had managed to be invisible for so long, could surely have found a way of bolting from his son's car at a red light or screaming for help. The fact that he did not do so is an indication of the ultimate triumph of his higher will over his lower will.

The higher will is how *Keter* operates in our lives. It governs our altruistic and self-sacrificing decisions. It seldom needs activation through coercion. It is most often spontaneous. Our lower will is its shadow side, distorted by rationalization, base emotions, and primitive needs, often leading to actions of which we are ashamed and for which we feel remorse. Unless we are sociopaths, it plays a major role in our nagging self-doubt and poor self-image. Much of the second half of this book teaches ways of dealing with our shadow side and of attaining integrity, healing, and empowerment.

CHOCHMAH: THE SECOND SEFIRAH

The Hebrew word *chochmah* means "wisdom." The *Sefirah* of **Chochmah** is the source and reservoir of all knowledge. However, it is not merely a reservoir of divine wisdom, but also God's instrument for transmitting that wisdom as insight or intuition. Its transmission is experienced as a sudden, often unexpected flash of light in the darkness, in moments of inspiration and creativity.

Like *Keter*, *Chochmah* is first manifested in Creation. Following the awakening of the Divine Will, a general idea flashed through the Divine Consciousness about how to actualize the Divine Will to create. Without this, Creation would not have been possible. It was of this that the psalmist sang when he declared, "You have made all of them [the works of creation] with *Chochmah*" (Ps. 104:24).

Because *Chochmah* is one of our spiritual building blocks, it is also responsible for human insights and intuitions. Thomas Kuhn implies this in his groundbreaking book *The Structure of Scientific Revolutions*. Great progress, he asserts, does not occur in orderly stages. It emerges through flashes of intuition that come to intellectual revolutionaries, apparently out of nowhere. The effect of these epiphanies is often the rejection of previous theories. Until somebody else experiences his or her own flash of intuition on that topic, a generation or so of scientists will simply tweak the original idea, refining and milking it to yield further benefits.

Revolutionary insight that is mediated by *Chochmah* is not contingent upon the usual rational processes of logical thought. It is a gift, an act of grace. It is the "Eureka!" of an Archimedes in the moment that he discovered the law of specific gravity. It is the "Aha" of a Newton, who, in the moment that he saw the legendary falling apple, changed physics forever through his discovery of the law of gravity.

Nobody will dispute the scientific contributions of Albert Einstein. Few people, however, know about their source. Somebody close to Einstein's colleague Professor Abe Gelbart has told the story of a conversation between the two men. Einstein had written and rewritten mathematical formulas for weeks on end, and nothing he did could resolve the problem. Then, one day, he was walking with Gelbart on the campus of Princeton University. Gelbart recalled that they were discussing many different things and that Einstein did not mention his insoluble problem. Suddenly, Einstein stopped in his tracks, an excited look on his face. "Abe," he exclaimed, "I've got it. It suddenly all makes sense to me. I see the whole thing totally differently."

Gelbart did not understand what Einstein was saying. "What are you talking about? What have we been discussing that has not been clear until this moment?"

Einstein then told his friend about his frustration, and how a sudden understanding had flashed through his mind, when he was not even thinking about the problem.

The insights of *Chochmah* are not limited to scientific breakthroughs. They happen in every area of human creativity. *Chochmah* was the source of deaf composer Beethoven's experience of hearing an entire symphony in a flash; of Wordsworth's reverie while sitting near Tintern Abbey in England and being moved to write "Lines Composed a Few Miles Above Tintern Abbey," one of the masterpieces of world literature; of Michelangelo's inspiration when the image of the creation of Adam flashed in his mind before he executed his immortal artwork in the Sistine Chapel.

I am nowhere in the league of these creative giants, but, like all of you, I have experienced moments of creativity. I always think my sermons and lectures through very carefully. Before I face a congregation or an audience, I have a clear succession of ideas in my head. Yet something often happens to me while I am speaking. The words seem to pour out of me and I lose ego awareness. I no longer even hear the sound of my own voice. When this happens, I am at my very best, but I am also at my most humble, knowing full well that I cannot take any credit for my "performance," that the rush of ideas and words was an unexpected gift from God through *Chochmah*.

Chochmah functions in human beings through the *Neshamah*. You will recall that our *Neshamah* is partly embodied and partly transcendent, the antenna that connects us to the collective wisdom of our people and humankind. It channels the intuitions that spark our creative cognitive processes, which have been dubbed our "right-brain" activities. It is not surprising, therefore, that the Kabbalah associates *Chochmah* with the right side of our brain. Neuropsychiatrist and neuroscientist Mona Lisa Schulz has largely validated that association in *Awakening Intuition*, her innovative exploration of the neurological processes that mediate our intuitions. Later, we shall discover how to awaken our intuitive sense and gain access to *Chochmah*.

BINAH: THE THIRD *SEFIRAH*

The Hebrew word *binah* means "understanding," in the sense of analytical thinking or deductive analysis. *Chochmah* presents the mind with powerful but somewhat amorphous general ideas. For those ideas to become intelligible, they must be refined through rigorous analysis and broken down into component parts.

Like *Keter* and *Chochmah*, **Binah** is initially manifested in the Creation. The Kabbalah wrestles with a conundrum. If God is infinite, what "room" is there for anything he creates? The Kabbalah solves the riddle by having us imagine that Being willingly imposes limits on itself, contracting, as it were, to create space for the cosmos to occupy. This divine process of contraction is called **tzimtzum.** The will to create awakens within the divine essence

(Keter), and the grand vision of the cosmos flashes through the Divine Wisdom *(Chochmah)*, but its execution requires contraction and limitation *(Binah)*.

The *Sefirah* of *Binah* functions in more or less the same way in humans. The insights that come to great scientific minds must be contracted to mathematical formulas that can be understood by colleagues and students before they can gain acceptance. The soaring sounds heard by Beethoven in the moment of inspiration must be reduced to musical notation, edited, and revised to ensure their coherence and effect, and only then presented to musicians for execution. The process of analysis, revision, and editing may require a genius to discard elements of his or her original general intuition, and reorganize what is retained in a meaningful manner. In other words, *Binah* places limits on *Chochmah*.

A concrete example of this process may help. When people want to build a house, they have a general idea of how they would like the house to look. If they are serious, they employ an architect to help them translate this into reality. The architect considers the dream and asks the dreamers, "What's your budget for this project?" The clients answer, "Two hundred fifty thousand dollars."

The architect smiles and says very gently, "Your dream house will cost a million dollars more to build than you budgeted for. You have to limit the size of the house and the materials you'd like to use if you want to stay within your original budget." She continues, "I'm sure you're not aware of all the municipal ordinances that govern setbacks, the removal of trees, and the portion of the property on which the house may be built."

The clients gasp, "What else do we need to know?"

The architect continues, "Your vision exceeds government building limits on your land."

The dreamers are taken aback. "How much more do we need to cut?" they ask.

"That," she answers, "depends on the engineer."

"What do we need an engineer for?" the clients ask.

"The engineer considers additional factors," she replies. "How the water table of your lot will affect your choice of materials and even the feasibility of building according to my blueprint, how vulnerable the building will be in an earthquake, and how the plans need to be changed."

One of the tasks of the architect and the engineer is to place limits on the grand design once they have taken all factors into consideration. This is precisely the function of *Binah*. Without *Binah*, the marvelous insights of *Chochmah* will go nowhere. While *Chochmah* is limitless, *Binah* is limiting. While *Chochmah* is effortless inspiration, *Binah* is hard work and perspiration. A great idea needs to be thought through carefully before it can work in practice.

By the same token, unless there is *Chochmah*, a great idea, all the analysis of the most agile of minds is in vain. Although *Chochmah* and *Binah* are polar opposites, they are completely interdependent. Productive thought requires *Chochmah* and *Binah* to function in harmony and to be in balance. *Chochmah* and *Binah* together are two of the building blocks for the cognitive tasks of the *Neshamah*.

Whenever *Chochmah* and *Binah* are not integrated, we can expect problems. Mary and Simon's experience will show you what I mean.

MARY AND SIMON'S STORY

Mary and Simon came to me because their marriage was in trouble. It did not take long for me to get to the root of the problem. They were very different people with very different thinking styles. Simon was a mathematics professor at a leading university. Like most scientists, his *Binah* faculty predominated: he was analytical and rational. Although he was religiously observant, he had little patience with the supernatural and mystical dimensions of faith and considered them outmoded, primitive superstitions. He was impatient with processing feelings, and viewed problems as requiring rational solutions. On the other hand, Mary's religious faith centered around its mystical dimension. She was highly intuitive and had learned to trust her gut. Her husband's dismissive attitude to her belief in the supernatural and her need to process her feelings had led to frequent fights. While Simon was predominately *Binah*-oriented, Mary was predominately *Chochmah*-oriented.

Their conflict came to a head when Mary became ill and the accepted medical interventions failed to provide relief. Simon was convinced that her illness was "in her head" because no reliable diagnosis had been made. But Mary's gut guided her to a physician who practiced both traditional and alternative medicine. Predictably, Simon was scornful and sarcastic about her decision.

In therapy, Mary came to recognize that she was overly *Chochmah*-oriented and that her *Binah* needed developing. She enrolled in a graduate program, eventually earning a doctorate for a fine, well-researched study.

Simon was less open to change. He was reluctant to surrender his position that ideas that could not be proved must necessarily be false, until a family tragedy shattered his certainties. His elderly aunt was scheduled to fly in for a visit, but had called to tell him she was canceling her plans because she had had a premonition that something bad would happen if she made the journey. Simon persuaded her to put her anxiety aside, explaining it away as the fear of flying experienced by many infrequent fliers. But her taxi was involved in a collision on the way to the airport and she was killed. Simon could have put the accident down to coincidence, but did not, conceding instead the truth of Shakespeare's statement that "there are more things in heaven and Earth . . . Than are dreamt of in your philosophy" (*Hamlet,* act 1, sc. 5). His aunt's death was a wake-up call. He went into therapy to deal with guilt and depression. Simon's therapist also helped him confront his stubbornness, and he eventually agreed to join Mary for spiritually oriented couples counseling with me. After a few joint sessions, I invited Simon to work on awakening his *Chochmah.* His openness to the process brought him closer to Mary, eventually enabling them to find spiritual and emotional common ground.

People who are trained to use logic are often skeptical of the paranormal, and defend their presuppositions about critical and accurate thinking by performing all kinds of mind games to explain away phenomena that defy empirical proof.

My public teaching once earned me the scorn of a *Binah* personality of this kind. As part of a series of lectures I was giving on psychology and Kabbalah in London, I described the near-death experience, and a woman who had been sitting at the back of the hall raised her hand.

"Rabbi Weiss," she began, "I think you're misleading people with your mumbo jumbo. I'm a physician and know there is no empirical basis whatsoever for your claim that the so-called near-death experience can validate belief in personal immortality. You don't know what you're talking about and should confine yourself to preaching the Bible."

"But what about the research of such eminent psychiatrists as Moody, Ring, and Morse?" I asked. "Are their views also mumbo jumbo? What about the universal and cross-cultural reports about the characteristics of the near-death experience? How do you account for the story of the Russian physician's vivid description of his own near-death experience, despite his atheist education and his previous conviction that there is no such thing as a soul?"

Her response was uncomfortably patronizing. "My dear rabbi," she began, "have you not heard of a magazine called the *Skeptic*? Its contributors are all hard-nosed scientists. In a recent issue, an article appeared that debunked the whole near-death-experience hypothesis."

I led her on. "And how precisely did these scientists account for the out-of-body experience of people who had been diagnosed as clinically dead? How were so many of them able to describe in detail what was happening around their allegedly dead bodies, the conversations of the physicians and nurses, and so on? If there were no vital signs and if they had been diagnosed as dead, why were they able to give such accurate descriptions? How could dead people enjoy consciousness? Why is the experience of passing through the tunnel of light so widespread? Why is the rapid replay of their lives in the presence of a spiritual figure so common to those who have had the near-death experience?"

"It could be any number of things," she responded. "First off, the diagnosis of death must have been mistaken. Oxygen starvation may explain the out-of-body experience. So may their medications. The perception of light may be random firing of neurons in the brain due to causes not fully understood. The rapid replay of a lifetime of experience may have been a pure flight of fancy, influenced by reading and expectation. Many scientists have suggested a variety of explanations for the phenomena you've described."

Unbeknownst to me, Antonia Mills and Steven Jay Lynn had raised red flags of their own in their chapter on past-life experiences in *Varieties of Anomalous Experience: Examining the Scientific Evidence.* But I had still remained more convinced by the first-person reports of near-death experiences than by the explanations of the phenomenon. Therefore, I persisted.

"Strange," I said. "In my doctoral training in psychology— and it was rigorously scientific—I was always conscious of the principle of parsimony. May I explain that principle, not to you, Doctor, but to members of the audience who may not have our shared background in scientific method? The principle of parsimony is that a simple explanation that is sound is always preferable to more complicated and convoluted explanations. The simple explanation of the near-death experience is that it is what people say it is. The convoluted explanations are the unproven hypotheses of people, such as the contributor to the *Skeptic* you have cited, who do mental handstands to avoid acknowledging the supernatural. Critical thinking is necessary. But it cannot explain away uncomfortable phenomena."

My argument would have been bolstered by Bruce Greyson's study of the near-death-experience literature in *Varieties of Anomalous Experience.* Greyson examines a variety of hypotheses that have been presented to explain this phenomenon—psychological, physiological (anoxia), similarity to acceleration-induced loss of consciousness, and neurobiological. He argues that none of these is persuasive:

> To the extent that these psychological and physiological hypotheses succeed in explaining NDEs, they do so by focusing selectively on certain features of the experience and by declaring other features they do not explain to be peripheral to the phenomenon. No theory has yet been proposed that can account satisfactorily for all of the com-

mon elements of NDEs . . . None have been demonstrated to occur in a near death state and some, such as those based on cerebral anoxia, have been contradicted by empirical data. (pp. 336–337)

Unfortunately, I was not aware of Greyson's study at the time.

DA'AT: THE HIDDEN *SEFIRAH*

I have already pointed out that *Keter* is essentially incomprehensible. It throws light on the cognitive process only to the extent that it accounts for the act of will that precedes all human thought. Indeed, many kabbalists make little reference to *Keter,* and point to another *Sefirah* in the Tree of Life that more fully explains the human cognitive process.

Figure 5 shows the *Sefirah* of **Da'at.** To indicate that it is the "hidden *Sefirah,*" I have not shown its connections to the other *Sefirot.* This emphasizes that *Da'at* does not exist as a full *Sefirah* in its own right, but is that aspect of *Keter* that is accessible to human cognition and experience. *Keter* is the internalized, hidden will or desire, whereas *Da'at* is the externalized will or desire. Like *Keter, Da'at* is actually directly linked to *Chochmah* and *Binah* and facilitates their activities, but because it is an aspect of *Keter,* it is regarded as hidden.

The Hebrew word *da'at* is translated as "knowledge." It is knowledge that connects knowers to what they know. I was reminded of this in my work with Howard.

HOWARD'S STORY

Howard, who was a tenured biochemistry professor, came to me for help in dealing with his depression. He slept badly,

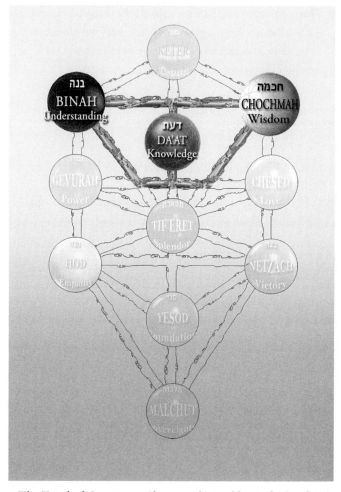

5. The Triad of Cognition, Showing the Hidden Sefirah of Da'at

because of his inability to stop repetitive thoughts. Not surprisingly, waking up in the morning became increasingly difficult. There were other telltale signs of depression. He had lost interest in many things that used to excite him. He occasionally missed important faculty meetings and would often not show up to teach his classes. He was losing weight and was more and more grumpy with his wife and children.

Howard frequently complained about his peers at the university and was beginning to believe that they did not want him as a colleague, even though they could not deny the importance of his work. Whenever we discussed the university, his depression became more palpable.

My initial assumption was that Howard had lost his passion for research and that he had become bored with what he was doing. I wondered aloud whether this was true and whether he was depressed because he was stuck in a profession that offered him no gratification. Howard was astonished by my suggestion.

"Never," he declared passionately. "It is my joy. It is my life. My every fiber resonates with what I am doing. I experience a fresh flush of excitement whenever my presentations are acclaimed at international conferences and my papers published in respected journals."

He was telling me that biochemistry was more to him than a mere body of knowledge. He was deeply committed to it and did not feel separate from his knowledge. It was part of his very being. Howard's attachment to biochemistry was a striking example of *Da'at* at work.

Yet if his profession was not his problem, what was depressing him? Eventually, we discovered that he felt a spiritual void. Passionate though he was about biochemistry, he needed something more. He told me that he wanted his life to make a difference to the Jewish people. This was the ancillary calling that had remained unconscious. Ultimately, Howard applied for a professorship at an Israeli teaching and research center. When he was accepted with immediate full tenure, and when his family began to show enthusiasm about the move, Howard's depression lifted. The promptings of his *Da'at* had been validated. He had achieved the fulfillment for which he yearned.

The notion of *Da'at* as commitment and connectedness governs the relationship of Adam and Eve. The Torah tells us that "Adam knew *[yada]* his wife Eve" (Gen. 4:1). The reference is to physical intimacy, as is clear from the context. The Bible does not usually mince its words. In other places, the scriptural description of the sex act is graphic. The Bible calls intercourse "a flowing of the seed." When husband and wife sleep together, seed passes from one to the other. So why the self-censorship in the case of Adam and Eve? Obviously, the answer is that their union is described here as "knowledge" *(da'at)* because their relationship transcended the merely physical. It was the desire of a soul for its twin. It was soul connection—relationship and commitment. The word *da'at* conveys all these things.

My wife's doctoral dissertation in clinical psychology identified the most significant characteristics of the soul-mate relationship. Couples, whose relationships were defined by these characteristics, described the transcendent nature of their physical union. Using different words and imagery, they all described their joining as a profound knowing that two halves had become a whole, and that a lost part of themselves had been recovered. It was as if each had come to know himself and herself as well as the beloved other. Furthermore, every couple described a spiritual energy that they felt surrounding them. Each of the couples was reliving the Adam-and-Eve experience of loving as knowing.

How does *Da'at* function together with *Chochmah* and *Binah*? *Chochmah* is a general insight. *Binah* is the process of analysis, refinement, and limitation of the general idea. But analysis can be endless. Ideas have infinite permutations and can be taken apart in myriad ways. The process of cognition is completed only by a commitment to a particular analysis. At this point, *Da'at* represents the will to translate an idea into action. It is in this sense that *Da'at* emerges from *Keter* and creates a transition between thought and action. The first triad can, therefore, be viewed in two ways. The first conceals *Da'at,* and the second allows it to emerge as the final stage of the cognitive process, the stage of decision and commitment.

Analysis and intuition are part and parcel of the cognitive process, and the function of *Da'at* is to create harmony between them. *Chochmah, Binah,* and *Da'at* need to be in balance. If they are not, our thought processes become dysfunctional.

The Kabbalah calls the three *Sefirot* of cognition ***mochin,*** from the Hebrew for "brain." It also uses the initial letters of *Chochmah, Binah,* and *Da'at* as an acronym for the *Sefirot* that govern thought **(ChaBaD)**. It is interesting to note that **Chabad,** founded by Rabbi Schneur Zalman, the **Alte Rebbe** (1745–1813), and certainly the most influential group within **Chasidism** today, has taken this acronym as its name. Its mission is to translate the divine master plan for mankind into practical projects. Is it too far-fetched to suggest that its leadership is the general contractor and that its emissaries worldwide are the specialized subcontractors for building the world in the image of God?

SUMMARY

Since human beings are incapable of understanding the concept of Creation out of nothing, the Kabbalah gives us an inkling of the process in its description of the first sefirotic triad. *Keter* is the stirring within the Divine that motivates the emanation of some-thing *(yesh)* from the ineffable infinite *Ayin* (No-thingness). The will to create requires a strategy for Creation, and this is the function of divine wisdom *(Chochmah)* and understanding *(Binah).*

The blueprint for all human thought processes is a function of the same *Sefirot*. *Keter* represents our will to be creative and to produce useful ideas. *Chochmah* is the vehicle for human intuition and creativity. Intuitions come to us unexpectedly, like flashes of lightning in a dark night. They are not the product of intellectual toil but, rather, an act of grace and require analysis, editing, and clear formulation. That is the function of *Binah*, or analytical intelligence. The products of *Chochmah* without the discipline of *Binah* are inchoate and sloppy. Analytical intelligence without inspiration is of limited use.

Chochmah and *Binah* were designed to function in harmony, which they do through the agency of *Da'at*. This is the externalized will that is responsible for our commitment to what we learn and know. *Da'at* is also the bridge between the *Sefirot* of thinking and the *Sefirot* of feeling, between the *Neshamah*, or cognitive element of our souls, and the *Ru'ach*, which governs our emotional faculties.

Painful childhood experiences can throw the *Sefirot* of thought out of balance. The resulting disharmony sometimes affects our *Keter*, and we substitute selfish motives for altruistic ideals. Sometimes our *Chochmah* is affected, and we become disorganized, using our bohemian, nonconforming personalities to justify avoiding responsibility and making commitments. Sometimes *Binah* is distorted. If this happens, we may become know-it-alls and play mind games to avoid facing our true feelings. Many people suffer from problems that relate to their *Da'at*. They are chronic procrastinators and commitment-phobics.

Fortunately, the problems of unbalanced cognitive energy can be fixed. You will soon learn how such problems develop and effective techniques for remedying them.

6

THE SPIRITUAL GENOME:
HOW WE FEEL

———◆◇◆———

I have described the role of *Da'at* as the interface between think-ing and feeling. We need commitment, effort, determination, enthusiasm, and, sometimes, sacrifice to implement our ideas suc-cessfully. The three *Sefirot* that govern emotion control our passion and excitement, and motivate us to succeed. The Kabbalah calls this triad **ChaGaT,** the acronym for *Chesed, Gevurah,* and *Tif'eret.*

CHESED: THE FOURTH *SEFIRAH*

The word *chesed* means "love without limits." Like *Chochmah,* under which it is located in the kabbalistic Tree of Life, ***Chesed*** reflects God's grace. It is the unconditional outpouring of God's kindness. It is limited neither by the character of the recipient nor by the sacrifice it requires of the Divine. In chapter 5, I described the doctrine of the contraction *(tzimtzum)* of Infinite Being to cre-ate "space" for the cosmos. The act of Creation required God, as it were, to sacrifice his limitlessness. Absolute love is impossible with-out sacrifice. The *Sefirah* of *Chesed* reflects the divine love that made possible the transition of the idea of creation into the act of Creation. It is, perhaps, for this reason that *Chesed* is also called *Gedulah* (Greatness).

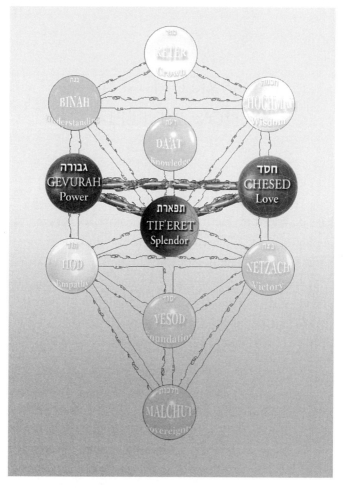

6. The Triad of Emotion

Chesed is the blueprint for all human loving and giving. It is limited neither by common interests nor by particular commitments. The psalmist knew what he was saying when he wrote, "The world is built on *Chesed*" (Ps. 59:3). Societies can be dominated by dictators and tyrants for decades. Their long-term endurance, however, is a function of the *Chesed* of benevolent governments and individuals.

The biblical patriarch Abraham personifies *Chesed*. His benevolence was the ethical expression of his theology and was exemplified by his offer of hospitality to Bedouin strangers who were not related to him by faith or family, and by his intercession with God on behalf of the inhabitants of Sodom and Gomorrah. Centuries later, the sages attributed the spread of Abraham's revolutionary ethical monotheism to his embodiment of benevolence.

Individuals with healthy and well-developed *Chesed* make a huge difference. However, like the other *Sefirot*, *Chesed* can be thrown out of balance. Later in the book, you will learn the complete dynamics that are responsible for distorting *Chesed*. For now, it is sufficient to say that a distorted *Chesed* causes great pain and suffering. This is what happened to Benjamin.

BENJAMIN'S STORY

Benjamin was a Holocaust survivor and belonged to a congregation I served as rabbi. Prior to the Nazi invasion of Poland, his life had been almost idyllic. The family business had prospered, his father had become the head of the local community, and his parents were the major financial supporters of their congregation and its religious educational network. Representatives of spiritual leaders of other villages, towns, and cities came to the family home for help, and there was a room in their home for wayfarers who could not afford to stay in a hotel. Benjamin, his four sisters, and his two brothers lacked for nothing. He had few bad childhood memories. His negative experiences stemmed from bullying by his gentile peers, but his father always pointed to his own success and insisted that generous living was more important than jealousy and hatred.

Unfortunately, the family's prosperity aroused envy. Despite his father's extremely fair treatment of the workers in his factory, some were anti-Semitic and resented his success.

When the Nazis came to town, Benjamin and his family were able to secure a hiding place in the countryside, but somebody informed on them to the Gestapo. In a moment, everything changed. The family was herded into a cattle car and transferred to Auschwitz. At the time, Benjamin was a strapping fifteen-year-old. After they arrived, he never saw his younger siblings again. His mother was moved to a women's compound and Benjamin and his father were assigned to a barrack. An outbreak of typhus killed almost everybody in that barrack, but somehow Benjamin and his father survived and did not succumb to malnutrition or their frequent beatings. They even survived the long march into Germany following the Russian invasion of Poland. Miraculously, they were reunited with Benjamin's mother in a German displaced persons camp. The father's mantra was that survival and reunion were the rewards of his lifetime of generosity. Benjamin's parents chose to remain in Germany, where they prospered and had more children. Eventually, his parents died at a ripe old age.

Benjamin had relatives who sponsored his immigration to the United States. At first, he did well, nursing the considerable fortune he had inherited. Then he invested much of his money in stocks, and when the market crashed in 1987, Benjamin and his family had to struggle for a living.

Benjamin was referred to me because he was haunted by guilt. As long as he had been able to help others, he felt that his survival was justified. But now that he could no longer support the organizations that turned to him for help, he felt increasingly guilty that he had lived and his siblings had not. Benjamin's father had instilled in his son the lesson that philanthropy was the best defense against anti-Semitism, and even the perils of Auschwitz. Benjamin's life had come to mirror that of his father. He was all *Chesed,* but his *Chesed* was not calibrated by his own needs. Jewish law provides that one should give no less than 10 percent and no more than 20 percent of one's after-tax income to charity, lest one is no longer able to provide for one's own family. However, Benjamin had always ignored these guidelines and tried to continue this, even when he was almost destitute, unable to exercise restraint. His philanthropy had become a primitive survival mechanism. Benjamin's *Chesed* had transformed itself into its shadow.

GEVURAH: THE FIFTH *SEFIRAH*

The Hebrew word *gevurah* is usually translated as "power," "strength," or "courage," but in Kabbalah, **Gevurah** also carries the sense of restraint. It is the antithesis of *Chesed,* which is defined by its limitlessness. *Chesed* can be overwhelming because it flows everywhere. *Gevurah* imposes order, and is the root of immutable natural law, setting boundaries for planetary orbits to prevent the collision of worlds and to protect landmasses from inundation. Cosmic *Gevurah* is, so to speak, the limitation that God places upon himself, compelling him to follow his own rules.

In the human sphere, also, *Chesed* without limit can be catastrophic. Rabbi Yechiel Barlev offers a fine example of this phenomenon. A son commits an infraction. The father loves his son and, therefore, wishes to teach him a lesson—for his own good. It is the will of the father to punish him *(Keter).* A general idea of the punishment arises in his mind *(Chochmah).* That idea is refined as he tailors the punishment to the infraction *(Binah).* He commits himself to carrying out the punishment *(Da'at).* If his *Chesed* were unrestrained by his *Gevurah,* the punishment would be limitless. The action that arose from his love for his son might actually destroy the boy. *Chesed* and *Gevurah* act as mutual checks and balances.

The rabbis attributed another important function to *Gevurah,* and defined it in this comment: "Who has *Gevurah?* One who conquers his impulse" (*Avot* 4:1). They thus extended its role from the interpersonal to the intrapersonal, from restraint in interactions with others to self-restraint.

The Kabbalah regards the biblical patriarch Isaac as the personification or archetype of *Gevurah* because his life was characterized by restraint. He submitted to being bound to the altar for slaughter, accepted the wife who was chosen for him, allowed her to make his son, Jacob, his spiritual heir, repressing his special love for Esau, the firstborn, and he redug the wells the Philistines had destroyed, always avoiding confrontation. His was a life of continued limitation.

Gevurah has two additional connotations. First, as the human counterpart of the divine energy of law and order, it is the building block of judicial institutions. A judge is often required to suspend feelings of compassion when he or she imposes a harsh sentence on a wrongdoer. For this reason, *Gevurah* is also called **Din** (Judgment). Second, *Gevurah,* by establishing boundaries, provides us with a sense of security. We retreat behind our walls and fences to feel safe from perceived threat. *Gevurah* energy governs human feelings of insecurity and fear. These two aspects of *Gevurah* are closely related. Institutions of justice are dedicated to keeping people safe. If there were no criminals and nobody to threaten our security, we would not require the protection of the law.

Love *(chesed)* and fear *(gevurah),* as experienced in retreat, are our primary emotions and all other emotions are derived from them. Consider a few examples:

> *Joy.* Joy derives from feeling completely loved and cared for and is also experienced in loving others. Reciprocated loving is among the most joyous of human experiences.

Sadness. Our greatest experience of sadness is loss of love, or the death of a loved one.

Terror. Terror is the exaggerated experience of fear. We deal with terror by devising defenses and establishing boundaries to keep out those who may hurt us. This results in our self-enclosure and withdrawal.

Awe. Children (and many adults) are in awe of the president of the United States. This is because, in comparison, they feel insignificant and he seems larger than life. Awe arises from an understanding of personal limitation and vulnerability, and is, therefore, clearly connected with fear.

Anxiety. We are anxious when we feel unsafe, because of our perceived collapse of our walls, psychological defenses, and coping mechanisms.

Here is an example of what happens when *Chesed* and *Gevurah* are thrown out of balance.

YASMIN'S STORY

Yasmin was born to well-to-do and highly respected parents. In her native Morocco, family ties and family loyalty were highly prized, but her father had frequent violent outbursts. He was a North African Dr. Jekyll and Mr. Hyde, adored for his caring behavior outside the home and feared at home. Yasmin's mother was completely dominated by her husband, and her siblings were terrified of him. They were severely punished for minor infractions and often brutally beaten. Their mother feared for herself and made no effort to protect her children. When Yasmin was nine years old, her mother told her in an unguarded moment that she was "an accident."

Her father had been critical of her performance at school. The only way of avoiding his anger was to excel, but nothing she did won her father's approval. "You'll never be anything," he would often shout at her. She still recalls his mocking comments about a dress her mother had let her pick out for a family celebration. Yasmin's grandmother was the only one she could turn to, yet when she most needed her support, the old lady was too frightened of her son to intervene.

Yasmin learned early on not to trust or rely on anybody. She left home, came to the United States, and enrolled in college. She sailed through college and her doctoral program, and became a professor of international relations at a prestigious university. However, despite her success, she was desperately unhappy. Although she was well educated, she still feared "the evil eye" and believed that any blessing she received would be taken away. She had not married because she was sure she was "bad news." "Anyway," she asked me, "how could I trust a man to be there for me always?" And, she added, "if by some miracle, someone wonderful will have me, something will happen to him, and I'll be even more hurt."

Yasmin had become all *Binah* and *Gevurah*. Her analytical acumen had enabled her to find flaws in all her suitors, and she described herself as a "male repeller." It was a great way of practicing one-upmanship and keeping her distance. She had wanted to be independent and had succeeded marvelously. She had convinced herself that she could neither receive nor give love. This told me that her problems were not limited to *Binah* and *Gevurah* but were also related to *Chesed*. With an atrophied *Chesed,* and her overly developed *Gevurah,* it made sense that Yasmin's relationships had all been short-lived. She was so well defended that nobody had been able to penetrate her defenses, and she had never been able to trust anyone.

TIF'ERET: THE SIXTH SEFIRAH

Tif'eret is usually translated as "beauty" or "splendor," but the kabbalistic understanding of the term goes way beyond its usual translation. As the divine energy that mediates between *Chesed* and *Gevurah*, it has three interrelated meanings—mercy, beauty, and truth. Strict justice rewards the winner and has no mercy on the loser. On the other hand, a judge's benevolence *(Chesed)* may result in injustice and resentment. Special consideration for the poorer of two litigants, for example, is deeply resented by his or her more affluent opponent. One's personal circumstances should not have any bearing on the judicial process. It is for this reason that Judaism prefers compromise to strict justice. When each litigant recognizes the needs and dignity of the other, the outcome demonstrates the quality of mercy. This is *Tif'eret* energy in action.

According to the Kabbalah, the harmonizing of polar opposites *Chesed* (loving-kindness) and *Din* (Judgment) is not merely compromise, but their synthesis. As the great Rabbi Judah Loewe of Prague pointed out, absolute opposites cannot coexist. Each threatens the existence of the other, and stability is achieved only by the introduction of a third harmonizing element. The third element contains the two opposites within itself, but is, at the same time, an entirely new force that is generated by them. Synthesis, thus understood, is the principle of development and growth. People who are familiar with the dialectical philosophy of Hegel will see that the Kabbalah predated his revolutionary idea of thesis, antithesis, and synthesis by many centuries.

The synthesis of *Chesed* and *Gevurah* allows the further movement of divine energy through the cosmos. The celestial quality of beauty is the new energy produced by this synthesis. To understand the emergence of beauty from these *Sefirot,* think of these opposites as black and white. You might think that the synthesis of black and white can only be gray, but anybody who is familiar with the art of black-and-white photography will tell you that a myriad of beautiful forms and images can emerge from shades and combinations of black and white.

Tif'eret is also the *Sefirah* of truth. *Emet,* the Hebrew word for "truth," begins with *aleph* and ends with *tav,* the first and last letters of the Hebrew alphabet. The middle letter of *emet* is *mem,* the middle letter of the Hebrew alphabet. Truth is thus seen as encompassing the entire spectrum of reality. It is not only black and white but also everything in between. According to the Kabbalah, the Torah contains the entire truth. Not surprisingly, therefore, the Zohar on Genesis 1:3 locates it in *Tif'eret.* Torah "was engraved there [in *Tif'eret*] to shine forth" (Zohar 1:16b).

Jacob personifies *Tif'eret.* As the third of the patriarchs, he synthesizes their opposite qualities. He combines the *Chesed* of his grandfather Abraham with the *Gevurah* of his father, Isaac. Jacob and Rachel fall in love at first sight *(Chesed).* Nevertheless, Jacob agrees to exercise restraint *(Gevurah)* by waiting seven years for the consummation of their love, and agreeing to labor a further seven years in payment to Laban for her hand in marriage. He has one deeply beloved daughter, Dinah *(Chesed).* After her kidnapping and rape, he again exercises restraint *(Gevurah).* During Jacob's encounter with his inner demons on the dark night of his soul, which the Bible portrays as his wrestling with an angel, his name is changed to Israel ("he who struggles with God"). His recognition of his true character after that self-transcending struggle transforms him into the archetype of truth. As the prophet Micah declares, "You give truth unto Jacob" (Mic. 7:20). For the Kabbalah, as for Jung, archetypes represent real psychospiritual energies and are not merely literary devices. Thus, the children of Israel, Jacob's descendants, are spiritually rooted in him and, therefore, in the *Sefirah* of the Torah of truth, from which they draw direction and inspiration.

As with the other *Sefirot, Tif'eret* can also become distorted and be transformed into its shadow. Leonard's story is an example of the underlying psychospiritual dynamic of *Tif'eret* distortion.

LEONARD'S STORY

Like so many of us, Leonard had very critical parents who never hesitated to put him down, and, over time, he learned that it was not a good idea to confess his mistakes to them. He soon became a creative liar, training himself to remember every detail of his prefabrications to avoid being caught. His strategy was to create a veneer of perfection. As an adult, he was respected within his community for his generosity and the way he conformed to religious norms. Meanwhile, he had a string of affairs, cheated on his taxes, concealed income from his wife, and, on one occasion, left the scene of an accident. However, although Leonard had learned to get away with it successfully, he saw himself as an inauthentic person, a cheat, and a hypocrite, always on the verge of exposure.

Leonard's behavior reflected dysfunctions in all his *Sefirot* of feeling. His egocentric strategies were evidence of the distortion in his *Gevurah*. His inauthentic charity, with pledges made only to enhance his standing in the community, and his inability to maintain marital fidelity were evidence of the distortions in his *Chesed*. His hypocritical demonstration of care for the needy and the mind games he played with his wife showed me just how badly his *Chesed* had been affected by his defense strategies. As the synthesizing energy of his dysfunctional *Chesed* and *Gevurah*, Leonard's *Tif'eret* had become its own shadow, expressing itself in his dishonesty.

SUMMARY

A world without law and boundaries would rapidly disintegrate in chaos. The movements of the celestial bodies, ocean currents, and so on conform to natural limitations. Human society, too, is governed by laws. The restraints of natural and human law are functions of the *Gevurah*. But a universe governed exclusively by law would leave no room for miraculous acts of divine grace or transforming gestures of human love, sacrifice, and concern. *Chesed* is the necessary counterbalance to *Gevurah*. Furthermore, without truth and beauty, the universe and human society would lack inspiration. *Chesed* and *Gevurah* need to merge in *Tif'eret*.

The *Sefirot* of feeling—*Chesed, Gevurah,* and *Tif'eret*—operate in perfect harmony. Human beings, too, are created with these building blocks of their *Ru'ach* in balance. However, inappropriate decisions and choices upset that balance and are responsible for our dysfunctional ways of feeling. Life's challenge is to maintain the balance and, when necessary, to restore it.

7

THE SPIRITUAL GENOME:
HOW WE RELATE

—◆◇◆—

Netzach, Hod, and Yesod govern our relationships, and their acronym is **NeHiY.**

NETZACH: THE SEVENTH SEFIRAH

The next facet of the Divine is the *Sefirah* of *Netzach,* which is located directly below *Chesed* on the Tree of Life. The Hebrew word *netzach* means "victory," and is derived from the Hebrew word **menatze'ach,** meaning "conductor" or "director."

Chesed, as you have seen, is unconditional love, bestowed everywhere and on everything. *Netzach* is focused love. Unfocused love can be ineffective. If you love everything equally, you are likely to love nothing in particular. The love that really "makes the world go round" is love that's built on enduring commitments and relationships. *Netzach* is love that is exclusively directed. *Netzach* energy governs our most important interpersonal relationships, such as the love of parent and child, and the love between a man and a woman. If I were asked to make a simple distinction between *Chesed* and *Netzach* on the level of human relations, I would use Martin Buber's distinction between "I-it" and "I-thou." *Chesed* is an I-it relationship. When I bestow my love indiscriminately,

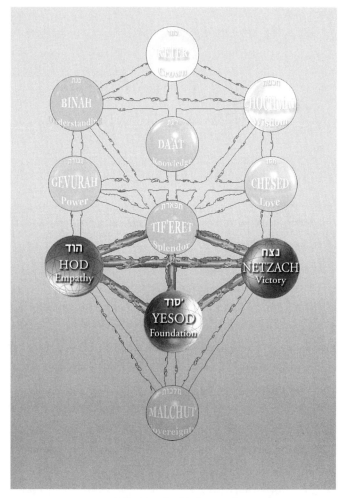

7. The Triad of Relationship

without entering into a special relationship with anybody, I don't address a "thou." I don't relate to another person but to an object that suits my personal agenda. That is why performing benevolent acts *(Chesed)* is relatively easy. Philanthropists do not have to be personally invested in the recipients of their benevolence. Indeed, they may themselves benefit directly or indirectly from their kindness, achieving prestige in their communities, and consciously or unconsciously satisfying their own ego needs. On the other hand, when I face the other person in the *Netzach* mode, I embrace a "thou." I embrace the singularity of the other when I focus my affection and loyalty on him or her.

But because *Netzach* is a divine energy, part of the spiritual DNA, it is not limited to human love and institutions. It also governs the love of a dog for its owner that is so often sacrificial and is always complete. As such, *Netzach* is embedded in all created things. Stated differently, *Netzach* is the spiritual root of the directed flow of love energy. It is in this sense that the Hebrew word *netzach* and the English word *director* are connected. Moses, the greatest of the prophets, facilitates the direct flow of divine love for humanity through the Torah. As the director of the Divine Will to Israel, Moses is the biblical personification of *Netzach*.

Like the other *Sefirot, Netzach* has its shadow side. Focused love may sometimes be exploitive and suffocating. In some of the stories later in the book, you will meet mothers whose conditional love for their children was their way of controlling their offspring. You will also meet a mother whose overprotectiveness crippled her daughter emotionally and a husband whose abuse of his wife stems from shadow *Netzach* energies.

HOD: THE EIGHTH *SEFIRAH*

Focused love is glorious. But it can also be dangerous. I may focus my love so powerfully on someone that I overwhelm him or her. In order to preserve the thou-ness of the other, the energies of *Netzach,* like the energies of *Chochmah* and *Chesed,* require restraint. *Netzach* energies are restrained by the *Sefirah* of **Hod.**

The Hebrew word *hod* means both "majesty" and "acknowl-edgment." In its direct linear connection to *Binah* and *Gevurah* (see Figure 1), *Hod* also reveals the divine energies of power and separateness. In that sense, *Hod* is majestic. But also like *Binah* and *Gevurah, Hod* is an energy of self-limitation. Let me explain this by redefining the concept of empathy.

Many books about the Kabbalah translate *Hod* as "empathy." Most people, including psychotherapists, understand empathy as a state in which someone is completely in tune with what another person is feeling. When therapists paraphrase what clients are say-ing, they call what they are doing "accurate empathy," which shows their clients that their feelings are correctly understood. Indeed, good therapists try to teach the technique of accurate empathy to clients who lack adequate communication skills.

But empathy, understood in this way, is by no means the exclu-sive domain of mental health professionals. We all try to be empathic. When I see a grief-stricken person who has lost someone very near and dear, and wish to comfort him, I say, "I empathize with you," trying to convey that I know exactly how he feels. Another example: I visit a patient in the hospital. She has had a ter-rible diagnosis, her prognosis is poor, and she is suddenly looking death in the eye. In an outpouring of empathy, I say, "I know just how you feel."

However, there is truly no way I can actually get under other people's skin and really know their feelings. Feelings are our own-most experience, and we experience them in a unique way. We can attempt to describe them to other people, but they will still not be able to experience them exactly as we do. When I say, "I empathize with you in your pain," what I really mean is that I have searched my memory for my own experience of pain and then imagined that your pain must be identical, all the while knowing full well that it is not.

So what is *Hod?* It can be translated as "acknowledgment." I fully acknowledge you only when I get out of your space, allowing you to be you—not part of my personal agenda or my ego projects. *Hod* is respect for the otherness of the other person. Many a writer of popular marriage manuals says of true love that two people can become one, claiming that one and one equals one. This equation is false both mathematically and existentially. One plus one always equals two. If two people could really be one, I would want to ask, "Which one? Who is incorporated by whom? Who is effaced by whom?" On the contrary, my relationship with another is meaningful only when I withdraw and allow my beloved to be other than I am. When that happens, one and one are truly two.

Unfortunately, like the other *Sefirot, Hod* energy has its shadow side. A person can withdraw to the point of becoming invisible in a relationship. Worse, by denying one's own uniqueness, one can permit oneself to be completely manipulated and exploited by the other. This is *Hod* energy at its dysfunctional worst, and was the spiritual root of Susannah's problem.

SUSANNAH'S STORY

Susannah had enrolled in one of my workshops. She had not actively participated in any of the group discussions or volunteered for any of the role-playing exercises. Then, suddenly, she became hysterical and bolted from the room. I followed her, while my copresenter continued to facilitate the rest of the group process. Susannah and I sat together for at least an hour. At first, the best I could do was to help calm her. Eventually, she shared her wrenching but all-too-common story with me. She had been sexually abused by her stepfather from age eight through adolescence. He had sworn her to secrecy, threatening to kill her and her mother if she ever breathed a word about it. She had ample reason to believe that her mother knew what was happening to her, but imagined that her mother was scared to rescue her. Susannah had spent many years in therapy, but had not been able to overcome her sense of shame or establish a fulfilling relationship with a man. The lesson she had learned growing up was that she was dirty, rotten, and unworthy. Her best defense was to "make no waves." The less she complained, the less complicated her life would be.

Susannah's experience is a textbook example of sexual abuse. The psychodynamics are clear. However, her wounds went far deeper, to her spiritual DNA, her dysfunctional *Hod*. Instead of merely allowing space for significant others to be themselves, she had taken the process to absurd lengths. She had withdrawn and had become psychologically and spiritually invisible. Her fear of making waves had transformed her into a doormat. She was used and abused by men time and time again, and was always disgusted with herself and never fulfilled.

It should not surprise you that Aaron, Moses' brother, is the archetypal embodiment of *Hod*. When Moses' return from Mount Sinai was delayed for forty days, the children of Israel became impatient and despairing. They asked Aaron to build a golden calf to replace their absent deity. He honored their request, repressing his own principles and personality. In his striving for peace, he denied his own spirituality and allowed himself to be exploited by the needs of those he sought to please.

YESOD: THE NINTH *SEFIRAH*

Like the other pairs, *Netzach* and *Hod* are opposites and are essentially unstable. They can survive only in synthesis, as a new revelation of divine energy called **Yesod,** meaning "foundation." In the example of the vision of a house and the various stages of its implementation, *Yesod* represents the laying of the foundations. It is the central pillar of all relationships, the dimension of connectedness with another person that spreads from *Da'at* along the trunk of the Tree of Life.

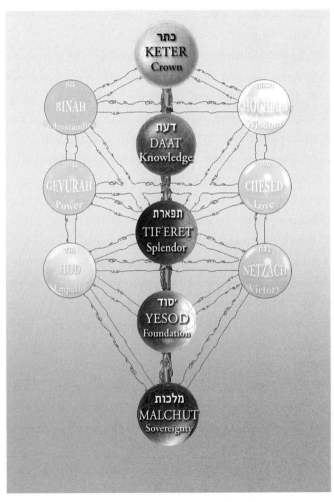

8. *The Trunk of the Tree of Life*

One of the configurations of the Tree of Life associates the *Sefirot* with different parts of the human body, and in it *Yesod* is always identified with the male sexual organ. At first glance, this association is startling. Human sexual activity appears to be no different from that of other animals. The visceral nature of sexuality explains why human sexual behavior is sometimes cruel, sadistic, or masochistic. Many religious traditions, therefore, contrast sexuality with spirituality and prize celibacy.

In contrast, Judaism considers sexuality sacred for both rabbis and laypeople, transforming it into an experience of transcendence. Indeed, the marital relationship is called **kiddushin,** a word derived from **kedushah** (holiness). Paradoxically, what can be the most animalistic of human activities is designated as holy.

The association of the *Yesod* with the male reproductive organ reflects the tension between animalistic and sacred sexuality. The male organ functions both as a channel for the elimination of waste and for the transfer of the seed of life. Sexuality can be crude and dirty. Sexual intercourse can be narcissistic, cruel, and, reflecting the shadow side of *Hod* energy, exploitive. The sexual partner can permit herself or himself to be reduced to an object. But the Jewish sexual ideal is its sanctification through committed loving. Sexuality can be loving and creative. The connection between *Da'at* and *Yesod* energies on the trunk of the Tree of Life highlights this notion.

You will recall that the Bible describes the sexual union between Adam and Eve in terms of *Da'at:* "And the man knew his wife Eve . . . and they became one flesh." In what way did Adam know Eve? Relationships can be characterized in terms of knowledge. The difference between an acquaintance, a friend, a special friend, a partner, and a spouse is a function of the degree of knowledge that defines the relationship.

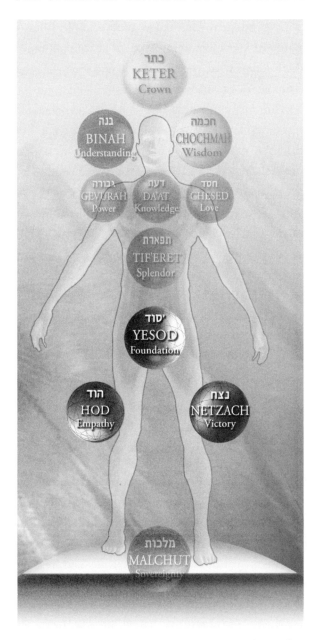

9. The Energy Centers Governing Human Relationships

If I have minimal knowledge about people, they are my acquaintances. I know something about them, but not much. I certainly don't know what their fears are nor their vulnerabilities, medical problems, or neuroses. I just have enough knowledge to identify them and plug them into a particular context. This is *Da'at* at its lowest level. People become my friends when I can trust them with some of my secrets and they can trust me with some of theirs. Nevertheless, our exchange of *Da'at* is incomplete. We do not trust one another sufficiently to feel safe and sure that what we reveal about ourselves will not be shared with others. In friendship, *Da'at* exchange is still compromised by fear.

A special friend is defined by a greater degree of *Da'at*. We trust a really good friend with our secrets. We take the risk of allowing our special friends to see us more as we actually are than the public face we show to the rest of society. My very closest friend is the person to whom I show most of my vulnerabilities, reveal most of my secrets, and share things about me that are generally hidden. The exchange of *Da'at* on this level has become commensurate with the growth of trust.

Some sibling relationships are characterized by a completely uncensored exchange of *Da'at* and are based on sacrificial giving, caring, and sharing. For example, a sibling who donates a kidney to his or her brother or sister exhibits a profound connection. Organ donation is reminiscent of Adam's gift of life to his Eve.

In many blessed instances, altruistic friendships have a similar level of intensity. The story of David and Jonathan is a case in point. The insanely jealous and insecure King Saul was concerned that David would usurp Jonathan's power after the king's death. To preserve his son's legacy, Saul planned to kill David, but Jonathan's love for his friend transcended self-interest. In a memorable exchange of *Da'at,* he revealed Saul's plan to David, risking his father's uncontrollable wrath.

The exchange of *Da'at* often occurs between loving spouses. In such cases, the beloved knows that the other will accept him or her in spite of weaknesses, vulnerabilities, and even some bad habits. The Bible commands, "Thou shalt love thy *re'a* as thyself" (Lev. 19:18). The word *re'a* is always translated as "thy neighbor." In my opinion, this translation is not entirely accurate. The Hebrew word for "friend" is **chaver.** The Hebrew word for "neighbor" is *shachen.* The word *re'a* is commonly used in the marital context. In the nuptial blessings, bride and groom are called "the beloved *re'im*" (the plural of *re'a*). The word *re'a* is related to the Hebrew word *ra'ua,* which means "unstable" or "broken." Husband and wife are thus called "the vulnerable ones." Understood in this way, the Bible commands us to love our marital partners, notwithstanding their vulnerabilities and shadows, in the same way that our healthy love of ourselves is not undermined by our own weaknesses.

A mature, committed relationship can persist after we have stripped away our public personae, allowing the beloved to see us as we really are. Our confident, mutual self-revelation is the fullest expression of *Da'at.* At that stage, nothing is kept hidden. Communication on the different levels of *Da'at* is finally consummated (summed up together) by communion: "And Adam knew his wife Eve . . . and they became one flesh." *Yesod* transforms communication into communion, and boundaries melt away. Neither party dominates the other. There is an exquisite oscillation between giving and receiving. He gives and she receives; she gives and he receives. The rhythm of the physical motions of lovemaking reflects the cycle of giving and receiving, the reciprocity and mutuality of loving.

But there is much more. In the moment of joining, it is as if a key has been turned in a lock that opens the heart. *Yesod* unlocks the energies of the focused love of *Netzach,* and the unconditional outpouring of *Chesed.* The experience of the beauty and harmony of committed physical union is *Yesod's* unlocking of *Tif'eret* energy. *Yesod* not only connects two people who love each other, but also connects them to *Havayah*. The Hebrew word for being together, **devekut,** describes both sexual union and the union of human beings with God.

It should come as no surprise, therefore, that Moses Maimonides, Judaism's greatest philosopher and theologian, uses committed sexual love as the paradigm for love of God. True soul mates often report that their act of making love opens a window to the Divine. The sages have said, "If husband and wife are worthy, they're enveloped by the Divine Presence" (*B. T. Sotah* 17a). Sexual union is actually transformed into a blessed moment of self-transcendence.

The Kabbalah regards Joseph as the embodiment of *Yesod.* Alone and alienated as a slave in charge of Potiphar's household, the handsome young Joseph was enticed by the seductive Mrs. Potiphar. He resisted her charms, even at the cost of his position, showing how raw sexuality can be constrained by noble principle. He was willing to wait for a wife with whom to attain *kiddushin.*

The Kabbalah interprets Jewish ritual circumcision as symbolizing the constraints that the human will places on sexual desire, transforming those energies into an expression of the sacred. Circumcision reveals the crown *(atarah)* of the male reproductive organ. *Atarah* and *keter* are synonyms.

The triad of relationship—*Netzach, Hod,* and *Yesod*—are the spiritual building blocks of the *Ru'ach* element of the human soul. The Kabbalah often calls the triads that govern feelings and relationships **middot** (virtues). Just as the human soul is created with the *Sefirot* of emotion in balance, its *Sefirot* of relationship are also balanced. Life's challenge is to maintain that balance. Both *Netzach* and *Hod* can become pathological and suffocating. Instead of recognizing otherness, an imbalanced *Hod* can lead to self-effacement and tolerance of abuse by manipulative partners. Loveless intercourse and exploitive sexuality, the shadow side of *Yesod,* cause massive imbalance in the *Sefirot* of relationship.

OTHER AUTHENTIC RELATIONSHIPS

When I share the implications of the kabbalistic triad of relationships at lectures, reactions are mixed. People who enjoy fulfilling marital relationships are inspired by the description of the holiness of *Yesod* sexual energies. Some who do not feel fulfilled in their marriages are motivated to work on transforming their relationships, either alone or with the help of couples' therapists. Later in this book, you will learn techniques for achieving marital transformation.

Some people live alone. The more spiritually inclined among these are at peace with their situation. They know that they are on a journey and that they chose the challenges of this particular incarnation before they were born. If their purpose on earth, their *tikkun,* is to learn the lessons of solitude, they are willing to do so. If they are to be reunited with their soul mates after this incarnation, they are ready to wait. Some of them are open to the possibility of unexpected change. Even after they may have abandoned hope of finding lasting marital fulfillment, their beloveds may suddenly enter their lives. Some have been deeply wounded by failed relationships and prefer living alone to risking further hurt. But many single people yearn for the kind of relationship I describe and are bitter that their hopes have been dashed.

I do not wish to give the impression that spiritual fulfillment and transcendence are exclusively dependent on the exchange of *Yesod* sexual energies with a beloved partner. The Tree of Life consists of three triads, and each provides a blueprint for significant living. The exchange of *Yesod* energies is not the only path to spiritual transformation.

Let me begin with the first triad. Earlier, I mentioned theta meditation. Through regular practice, our brains can be entrained to this mode of receptivity, allowing us to enhance *Chochmah* energies. In rabbinic Hebrew, meditation is called **hitbodedut,** meaning "self-isolation." The beginning of the spiritual experience, therefore, does not require the presence or participation of others.

Many people find special meaning for their lives through charitable projects. For them, *Chesed* is the springboard to significance. When they befriend the needy and help lift the despair of the depressed, they move beyond the narrow circle of self into the realm of spirit. Philanthropy is a powerful segue into community.

But the development of our *Binah* faculties is best accomplished in fellowship. Judaism's emphasis on studying together points the way to a spiritually cognitive life. The Aramaic word for a study partner is **chevruta,** and the root of this word is *chaver* (friend). Relationships of great depth develop through common commitment to intellectual growth and discovery. Serious study is a path to self-transcendence, fellowship, and community.

Not long ago, three Islamist terrorists burst into the kitchen of the **yeshiva** in Otniel, Israel. A single door separated the kitchen from the dining room. Scores of young men were in the dining room at the time. An eighteen-year-old student happened to be in the kitchen when the terrorists arrived with machine guns blazing. The young man could have dashed through the door, possibly saving his life under one of the tables in the dining room, or by being shielded by fellow students from the hail of bullets. Instead, he chose to remain in the kitchen, blocking the doorway, in the hope that the shooting in the kitchen would be heard by the guards outside before the murderers reached the crowded dining room. He knew that his decision to remain behind would cost him his life, but hoped it would save the lives of his friends. The guards killed the terrorists before they could enter the dining room. The young man's sacrifice was an astonishing example of *Gevurah* energies. He had not yet found a life's companion, but can anybody argue that his life had been without significance? *Gevurah* energies do not always require the ultimate sacrifice. Lesser acts of self-restraint are also paths to self-transcendence.

Many people achieve self-transcendence through art, music, and writing poems, stories, plays, and books. The beauty and truth of their creations are a reflection of their personal spiritual energies. Just as these *Tif'eret* energies inspire others, they transform their creators. Their creativity gives meaning to their lives and joy to others.

I defined *Netzach* as loving focused on another person with whom an ongoing "I-thou" relationship is established, but this does not always involve sexual intimacy. It can be a deep connection between parents and children, grandparents and grandchildren, brothers and sisters, spiritual leaders and their disciples, teachers and students, Big Brothers and their "sons," and so on. But the singular "I-thou" connection is not the only expression of focused loving. *Netzach* is also the love of a Mother Teresa for the poorest of the poor. It is the love of an Albert Schweitzer for the lepers in Africa. It is the love of a Florence Nightingale, whose life was dedicated to nursing soldiers during the Crimean War. This kind of relational energy is clearly transformative.

Hod energy governs our ability to recognize and honor the uniqueness of other people. This vital element of relationships is nothing less than the recognition of the image of God. Contemporary philosopher Emmanuel Levinas has called our acknowledgment of the other an epiphany, a mode of self-transcendence. In this way, the cultivation of *Hod* becomes an act of worship.

Yesod is the consummation of all the triads of the Tree of Life. However, sexual energy is not its only expression. You will recall that Joseph was regarded as the personification of *Yesod,* and in rabbinic literature is called "the righteous one" *(ha-Tzadik)* despite his sexual self-denial. Rabbi Aryeh Kaplan puts it this way in *Innerspace:*

> We have seen that the **Tzadik,** the righteous person, represents *Yesod*—Foundation, and that in the World to Come, the Righteous will sit with "their crowns [*atarot*] in their heads" [*B. T. Berachot* 17a]. . . . In ancient kabbalistic texts, the word *Atarah* also refers to the crown of *Yesod* . . . As we saw from the verse "the righteous man is the foundation [*yesod*] of the world" [Prov. 10:10], the *Tzadik* represents *Yesod.* Hence, a *Tzadik* is somebody who can have Divine pleasure or pleasure from *Yesod* . . . The Righteous are portrayed with the attribute of *Yesod* in their minds. They derive pleasure from the radiance of the Divine Presence. This is essentially a *Yesod* relationship with the Divine. (p. 69)

Clearly, righteous living is, itself, a pathway to the Divine, establishing a *Yesod* relationship with the Infinite.

SUMMARY

The three *Sefirot* of feeling govern primary emotions and their general societal effects. *Chesed* is the spiritual root of love and mediates acts of loving-kindness, but is not necessarily directed to specific beneficiaries. Indeed, Jewish tradition values anonymous benevolence as the highest expression of *Chesed.* The shadow side of this *Sefirah* is suffocating concern for others or self-defeating sacrifice. *Gevurah* is the spiritual root of restraint and protectiveness, and accounts for the establishment of law and order in society and for the boundaries that individuals create to keep themselves safe. Its shadow is war, violence, rage, and dysfunctional defenses. *Tif'eret* synthesizes *Chesed* and *Gevurah* and is responsible for harmony, truth, and beauty. But when it is out of balance as a result of childhood or past-life experiences, it accounts for hypocrisy, dishonesty, and disregard for the needs of others.

Together, the *Sefirot* of feeling and *Netzach, Hod,* and *Yesod,* the *Sefirot* of relating, are the building blocks of the *Ru'ach* element of the human soul. However, the *Sefirot* of feeling are distinguished from the *Sefirot* of relating in a fundamental way. To borrow philosopher Martin Buber's phrase, the *Sefirot* of feeling govern "I-it" relationships rather than "I-thou" relationships. Just as the highest level of philanthropy is anonymous, true justice is blind and not influenced by personal considerations. Judges who have personal relationships with litigants are expected to recuse themselves. Truth must not be compromised by personal prejudice and commitments to other interests.

In contrast, *Netzach, Hod,* and *Yesod* define authentic "I-thou" relationships. *Netzach* governs the love of a mother for a child, a husband for a wife, a teacher for a student, and so on. *Hod* is at the root of our acknowledgment of the otherness of another person and prevents us from engulfing that person entirely. It enables that person to maintain his or her own boundaries. When *Netzach* and *Hod* are balanced, loving partners perform a dance of giving and receiving, of being alternately active and passive. This dance usually manifests as great physical intimacy, which is the function of *Yesod*.

Unfortunately, the *Sefirot* of relationship can be thrown out of balance as a result of bad experiences. The defense mechanisms put in place by those who have been wounded often produce consuming spouses and manipulative parents, indications of *Netzach* dysfunction. Codependent behaviors are rooted in *Hod* dysfunction. People who remain in abusive relationships are afraid to be themselves and assert their own needs, because they consider divorce a failure, are afraid to be alone, or anticipate serious injury if they leave. Persistently unsatisfying sexual relationships can be traced to *Netzach* and *Hod* imbalance that expresses itself in unfulfilling and sometimes humiliating *Yesod* behaviors.

8

REPAIRING THE WORLD

———◆———

MALCHUT:
THE FEMININE ASPECT OF DIVINITY

The nine *Sefirot* I have described are channels for and facets of divine energy. Each is an aspect of the divine light and plays an active role in the process of creation. The tenth *Sefirah*, **Malchut** (Sovereignty), is completely passive.

In itself, *Malchut* possesses nothing, but merely receives the energies of the nine higher *Sefirot*. It has been compared to the moon, which is not an independent source of illumination, but reflects the light of the sun and transmits it to the earth. Similarly, *Malchut* receives its spiritual energy from the other *Sefirot*, and passes the abundance it receives to all created things. Put differently, it is the "root" of created things, receiving and channeling all the divine energy that reaches them. As such, it is the final spiritual building block of our tangible universe, the realm of *Asiyah*.

The six *Sefirot*, ChaGaT and NeHiY, are active energies, the divine qualities of masculinity. In contrast, the tenth *Sefirah*, as the archetypal receiver, embodies the feminine principle. The Hebrew word *malchut* means "sovereignty" or "rulership." In most religions and cultures, leadership has been a male prerogative. Biology has

10. The Sefirah *of* Malchut

been destiny. The male reproductive organs are visible, and the female reproductive organs concealed. Thus the male embodies exteriority and the female modesty and interiority. The male role is public and the female private. The male is active, and the female passive. The male provides the seed, and the female receives it. The male dominates, and the female submits.

The Kabbalah rejects this perspective. The female is not merely a passive receptacle. Consider the physiological connection between the male and the female. The male produces a million sperm cells, and the female generally accepts only one of them. After she receives the contracted male life force, a new process begins. Conception triggers gestation. The combination of what she receives and what she already has engenders miraculous growth and development. And, in the end, she gives back infinitely more than she has received. The tiny sperm cell she accepted becomes a living organism, a newborn baby, an addition to her family and the family of humankind. As creator of life, the female is godlike. She is the spiritual fulcrum of the family, its real leader. Her husband's public role is limited by her needs.

Malchut, therefore, is the feminine aspect of the Divine. The Kabbalah calls the female energy the **Shekhinah**—the indwelling Divine Presence on earth. Simultaneously receiver and creator, the woman, like God, has both feminine and masculine attributes. Simultaneously outgoing and housebound, the male, also like God, has masculine and feminine characteristics. Both the man and the woman must acknowledge their masculine and feminine sides to function properly in the realm of *Asiyah,* since, ultimately, our society is the realm of shared responsibility.

THE COSMIC CONSEQUENCES OF HUMAN ACTION

The woman's giving more than she receives is the paradigm of the function of the tenth *Sefirah.* It channels the energy of the nine higher *Sefirot* into everything in our material universe, serving as the cosmic building block of inanimate, vegetable, animal, and human beings.

Malchut receives its energy through *Yesod,* while also transmitting energy back to *Yesod* and, through it, to the higher *Sefirot*. Every human act of loving-kindness, justice, and self-restraint generates an upward flow of divine energy and directly affects the entire Tree of Life. Human actions thus have a ripple effect on the *Sefirot* and have cosmic consequences.

God replicates the primordial process of *tzimtzum* in *Malchut*. In the words of Rabbi Aryeh Kaplan, he "constricts himself in order to give over his kingdom to humankind. He is essentially saying, 'I created the world in such a way that it is all up to you now. I am giving you the keys' " (*Innerspace,* p. 76). Humankind, through *Malchut*, becomes the partner of God in the work of Creation.

Malchut is personified by David, who, emulating God, handed his kingship to his son Solomon during his own lifetime. Paradoxically, David, a powerful male, personifies the feminine aspect of the Divine, because he is "the sweet singer of Israel," as well as a mighty king. Since *Malchut* is, initially, receptive, it is symbolized by the human mouth, and, specifically, in its archetypal form, by the mouth of the "Psalmist." As the "mouth," *Malchut* is also the *Sefirah* of the Oral Torah, which embodies our ongoing effort to decipher the divine will and make its implementation possible. Thus, mankind becomes God's partner, not only in the work of Creation, but also in the task of God's ongoing revelation.

MENDING THE WORLD,
MENDING OURSELVES

The Kabbalah asserts that God deliberately integrated limitation, imperfection, and evil into the cosmic blueprint. The possibility of choosing between good and evil is the foundation of the moral order, but according to the Kabbalah, the choice of good over evil transcends the framework of any human ethical system, and its effects are cosmic. The mystic masters use the metaphor of the "shattering of the vessels" to explain God's inclusion of evil in Creation. In their earliest emergence from *Ayin* in the universes that preceded even the realm of *Atzilut,* the Ten *Sefirot* were unconnected. Each was a separate vessel of light. The light was so intense, the energy so enormous, that the vessels could not contain it, and like a dam whose water has no way of flowing outward, the vessels shattered, and sparks scattered throughout the cosmos. Subsequently, the vessels were reconstituted by the Creator, and most of the scattered sparks of divine energy were relocated within them. At the same time, a mechanism was established for filtering, stepping down, and refracting the divine energy in a containable manner. Mending the vessels, gathering the sparks, and reconstituting the *sefirah* system in the Tree of Life took place in the universe of *Atzilut.* The newly interconnected *Sefirot* permitted the graduated and gradual flow of divine energy through the various universes until it reached this world of human activity.

However, the reconstituted *Sefirot* did not attain perfection. The effects of the primordial shattering of the vessels lingered, and it was left to humankind to complete the process of cosmic reconstitution. According to the Kabbalah, the human task is nothing less than **tikkun olam** (mending the cosmos). *Tikkun olam* is accomplished through the positive ways nations relate to one another, societies serve their members, people connect with other people, and through our striving for individual spiritual fulfillment. This is the purpose for which we are created and our moral and spiritual calling.

To understand how we are to accomplish this purpose, you need to know a little more about the broken vessels. Many **kelipot** (fragments of the shattered vessels) were not reintegrated into the newly reconstituted *Sefirot,* but remained scattered throughout the cosmos, eventually falling into our universe, the realm of *Asiyah*. Most of these *kelipot* contained trace elements of the harshest aspects of *Gevurah (sigei Gevurah)*. Effectively, almost completely devoid of divine energy and lacking even a trace of *Chesed,* God's attribute of loving-kindness, the *kelipot* became forces of darkness and evil. The Kabbalah calls these forces the **sitra achra** (the other side). Because the *sigei Gevurah* lack the energy to sustain them adequately, the dark *kelipot* are tenuously connected to Being, and attach themselves to things that are blessed with Being in order to survive, flourish, and grow. According to the Kabbalah, nothing on earth is as fully endowed with Being as the human soul. Therefore, when *kelipot* attach themselves to other living things, their permanent survival is not assured. Their connection to the immortal human soul alone guarantees their survival. The masters of the Kabbalah teach that when we connect with one another in loving ways, perform acts of loving-kindness, follow spiritual paths, and take steps to enhance our divine potential, the *kelipot* are unable to leech on to us and eventually cease to exist. But when we are hedonistic, selfish, exploitive, cruel, and conflictual, we invite their attachment to us. By consciously or unconsciously allowing ourselves to attract the *kelipot,* we sustain the *sitra achra*.

In its commentary on Genesis 1:5, the Zohar (1:17a) explains that conflict and disharmony are particularly effective in drawing and nourishing *kelipot*. This notion has special significance for kabbalistic psychology. Just as interpersonal conflict is a powerful magnet for *kelipot,* intrapersonal conflict, or inner disharmony, has the same effect. When dysfunctional patterns of thinking, feeling, and relating throw our delicate personal *sefirah* systems out of balance, our souls become encrusted with layers of *kelipot,* sometimes all but extinguishing our inner light.

The human task of mending the world is not limited to our

obvious encounter with the *sitra achra*. There is another category of *kelipah* that affects our spiritual health. Some *kelipot* are neither good nor evil and have the potential of going either way. The Kabbalah calls them **kelipot noga** (fragments with a significant residue of divine light). Because *kelipot noga* have traces of light, it is possible for human beings to release their concealed divine energy and to elevate it, transforming their potential for evil into good. How is this achieved? The Torah distinguishes between activities that are explicitly prohibited and those that are actually commanded. Consuming forbidden foods and harmful substances, having illicit sexual relationships, and committing robbery and murder exemplify activities that the Torah prohibits. The Kabbalah associates these activities with the *sitra achra*. People who indulge in them are magnets for dark *kelipot*. In contrast, for example, the Torah commands the consumption of matzot on Passover, and acts of benevolence and justice. The Kabbalah regards such commanded activities as good. Their performance shields us from the *kelipot,* making us more effective channels for divine energy, and increases the divine light in the cosmos.

However, there is a vast array of activities that are neither explicitly forbidden by the Torah nor commanded. The rabbis call this in-between category "permitted." For example, people are neither commanded by God to become information technology (IT) professionals nor prohibited from doing so. Information technology is neither intrinsically good nor evil, but has the potential of going either way. IT has been used by physicians to enhance their healing arts, and by researchers and ordinary people to communicate more easily and rapidly with one another. But it has also been used by hackers for theft and mischief, and by terrorist networks to spread death and destruction. Thus, IT exemplifies what the Kabbalah means by *kelipot noga*.

To cite another example, people are neither commanded by the Torah to eat peaches nor forbidden to do so. Therefore, peaches have the status of *kelipot noga*. We can choose to eat them for their nutritional value to help sustain our bodies as a temple for our souls. We can also enhance our sense of wonder at God's creation by contemplating the miracle of the form, texture, and taste of the peach, and by acknowledging this wonderful gift. These gestures transform the peaches we eat from neutral objects to holy things. In kabbalistic terms, the trace of light in the peaches is released, and the *kelipah* is elevated to its holy Source. On the other hand, we can choose to eat peaches because we are gluttons, simply because we like their taste or for their sensual gratification. By doing so, we fail to release the divine energy, and the *kelipah noga* becomes a dark *kelipah*, encrusting our souls.

Sexual relations, like eating and drinking, fall into "commanded," "prohibited," or "permitted" categories. The Torah commands us to marry and requires marital fidelity. Committed intimate relationships channel divine light and shield us from the encrustation of dark *kelipot*. The Torah prohibits, among other things, incest, pedophilia, adultery, and rape, not only because they are bad, but also because they encrust our souls with dark *kelipot*. However, even religiously sanctioned intimate connections have the potential of producing either good or evil consequences, placing them in the class of *kelipot noga*. People whose intimate connections are loving and respectful attract divine energy and elevate the *kelipot noga*. In chapter 13, you will learn how some people are able to achieve self-transcendence and have intimations of the Divine when they are joined to their partners. In contrast, rough, selfish, inconsiderate conjugal relations transform the *kelipot noga* into completely dark energies.

A story from my case files illustrates how dysfunctional and conflictual relations throw our *Sefirot* into imbalance and attract dark *kelipah* energies.

ANNA AND JACK'S STORY

Jack had a violent temper and often beat Anna. After one occasion when Anna was hospitalized, their physician referred them to me for marital therapy. Jack told me that after each assault on Anna, he was deeply remorseful: "I weep and feel sick to my stomach, and promise never to lay hands on her again." But as time passed, the anger rose again, and he would lose control, repeating the cycle of violence and remorse.

I asked Anna why she hadn't left him. "When Jack doesn't beat me, he's the most loving husband. His bitter tears tell me how much he really loves me and needs me. When he begs me not to leave him, I'm convinced of the depth of his love."

Jack's childhood had been turbulent. His father was a disciplinarian who practiced the proverb "Spare the rod and spoil the child." Jack had been severely punished even for transgressions of little consequence. His father's cruelty had made him increasingly angry, but fearing further punishment if he expressed his anger, Jack learned to contain his rage until, like an overinflated balloon, it would burst. His customary response to his violent loss of control was shame and remorse.

Anna's mother made it clear in word and deed that her love was conditional on her daughter's compliance with her wishes. It did not take Anna long to learn that good behavior and stoic acceptance of disappointment alone would ensure her mother's continuing love. To protect herself from loss of love, Anna had mastered the art of repressing her personal needs.

The Meaning of Jack and Anna's Story

Jack had become a classic dysfunctional *Gevurah*-oriented personality. He had learned to protect himself by withdrawing and containing his rage. But, like so many *Gevurah* types, his rage was not always containable, and he became prone to violent outbursts. His experience with his peers had confirmed that violence and remorse were an effective combination. People were afraid of him but did not end their friendship, because when he showed remorse, he was a loving and caring companion. However, it was not only Jack's *Gevurah* that was out of balance. The fact that Jack had became adept in exploiting his violence to dominate others also pointed to a severe *Netzach* distortion.

Because her love was exploitive, Anna's mother's behavior had reflected the darker side of her *Netzach* energy. In response, Anna marshaled dark *Hod* energies, transforming her into the family doormat. Anna had lost touch with who she really was and had come to deny her fundamental right to love and happiness.

The *sefirah* imbalances in Anna, her family, and her husband had become powerful magnets for the dark energy that increasingly disabled them.

The next six chapters of this book will help you diagnose the causes of different kinds of sefirah imbalance and teach you techniques for removing the *kelipot*. These explorations will help you to discover who you really are, which is a vital element in your personal *tikkun* and the repair of the world.

THE FAMILY

Families are small universes, and each has its *sefirah* system. The *Sefirot* of the family are its spiritual DNA. All families have spoken and unspoken rules that reflect the will of the head of the family. Sometimes family rules are transgenerational. In some, the rules are rigidly enforced, leaving little room for individual insight and exploration. These families suffer from *Binah* imbalance. In others, leaders govern by the seat of their pants. Their families suffer from cognitive chaos, reflecting the shadow side of *Chochmah*. In families with strong *Da'at* energies, the decision-making process is effectively geared to everybody's emotional needs. But in other cases, parents and/or children are unable to make and keep commitments, showing that their *Da'at* has become encrusted with *kelipot*.

Privacy is respected in well-adjusted families and members are given their own space, reflecting healthy *Gevurah* characteristics. However, sometimes, family boundaries are too rigid to permit strangers in and members out. They even keep parent away from child and child from parent. This is distorted *Gevurah*.

Chesed energies flow across all boundaries in families whose love is unconditional. Dysfunctional families, on the other hand, are sometimes torn apart by infidelities that are energized by dark, out-of-control *Chesed*. Families with healthy *Netzach* energies focus love appropriately. Everyone is made to feel special. But in other families, love is used for control. As in Anna's story, it is turned on and off to gain compliance. Healthy families encourage members to develop their own potential. Their specialness is nurtured and acknowledged. Their *Hod* is in balance. However, the dark *Hod* energies of dysfunctional families make some members invisible or, like Anna, victims of abuse. Children whose parents' *Hod* energies are *kelipah*-encrusted often become the carriers of family pathologies.

The mending of the world requires the removal of *kelipot* from dysfunctional families, because families whose *Sefirot* are in harmony become temples for the *Shekhinah*. God commanded Moses, "Let them make a sanctuary for me and I shall dwell in their midst" (Exod. 19:8). Note that the Torah does not say, "I shall dwell in it [the sanctuary]." It says, rather, "I shall dwell in their midst." This generates energies from *Malchut* to *Yesod* that rise to repair the cosmos as a whole.

The Berman family's story in chapter 14 will give you a good idea of how even extremely dysfunctional families can be healed and transformed.

SOCIETY

Benevolent societies provide networks of support for individuals, couples, and families. Institutions of *Chesed,* such as hospitals and social services, help injured people heal. Institutions of justice maintain boundaries. Offenders are punished and order is maintained. Societies, like families, have their rules, boundaries, and means of sharing and caring.

However, many societies are encrusted by evil. Their leaders incite true believers to steal, maim, and murder in the name of lofty principles. Suicide bombings and the rationalized slaughter of innocent individuals remind us that the world is still broken. Religious wars throughout the ages and the current acts of religious terror are part of a social order that needs redemption.

The Torah provides guidelines for fashioning society into the Kingdom of God. It insists that we protect the weakest and most vulnerable, extending *Chesed* to widows, orphans, and the disadvantaged. It establishes a system of justice that respects the needs of the individual, while also attending to the requirements of society as a whole.

However, mending the world begins with the mending of individuals and the development of functional, benevolent, balanced families. Ordinary individuals cannot declare war or make decisions that affect the world as a whole, or even the societies of which our families are a part. But we can control the way in which we live in the world, and the changes we make in the areas within our control have a ripple effect.

SUMMARY

Our actions have consequences. They impact our health, psychological well-being, and spiritual integrity. They affect our relationships and moral standing. They influence our communities, society, and, sometimes, our nation and the family of nations. According to the Kabbalah, the tenth *Sefirah, Malchut,* is a spiritual "switching system." This *Sefirah* is associated with the feminine aspect of divinity, the *Shekhinah.* Like a woman, who accepts a single sperm cell and gives back infinitely more than she receives in the form of a fully developed newborn, the tenth *Sefirah* receives the flow of divine energy through the Tree of Life before switching and reversing its flow back through the cosmos.

How we live and what we do are part of this spiritual feedback mechanism. It is related to the kabbalistic notion of evil and human free will. When we choose to live and behave with moral and spiritual integrity, we release the scattered divine sparks, and help eradicate evil from the entire cosmos. This process is called *tikkun olam* and occurs in the personal, family, communal, societal, and political spheres. However, when we choose not to be righteous, we nourish and reinforce the power of evil, both in the human realm and the cosmos as a whole.

9

WHY WE ARE UNHAPPY

———◈———

THE PSYCHOSOCIAL ROOTS
OF UNHAPPINESS

To a large extent, we are what we are because of the values of the societies into which we are born, and because of our family interactions. Some societies train us to hide our feelings. The ideal in those societies is to "keep a stiff upper lip," and people are regarded as weaklings if they acknowledge their feelings and vulnerabilities. The British society in which I lived for a brief but important period in my life epitomized the stiff upper lip. There, fewer people sought counseling than in the United States; they appeared to be reluctant, and, perhaps, even ashamed to share personal problems with others. In other societies, the expression of emotion is considered to be natural and healthy. The culture of the United States encourages the expression of feelings, and consultation with mental health professionals is widespread. People who seek psychological help are regarded as responsible rather than weak. It is considered irresponsible to neglect one's marital and individual emotional problems as it would be to neglect one's physical health. Some societies are authoritarian. They are governed by strict conventions, and people are expected to adhere to traditional roles and rules without question. The Western world was shocked by the absence of educational opportunities for girls and women in Taliban Afghanistan. Had we understood their particular Islamist culture better, we would not have been surprised. South Africa was particularly authoritarian. Laws made by the minority controlled the lives of the majority of the population. The questioning of those laws was both futile and dangerous.

Some societies, in contrast, are open and democratic. They invite participation in decision making, and freedom of expression is encouraged. Laws are fashioned by elected representatives. The questioning of authority is a sign not of rebellion, but of political maturity and responsibility.

As you have seen, the fundamental social unit of *Malchut* is the family. In many ways, the family mirrors the values of the society and the larger social groupings of which it is a part. Some societies and families regard education as fundamental. Children are encouraged to do well at school and witness their parents' love and commitment to intellectual growth and development. In other families, children grow up in homes that do not have books. Their parents show little interest in their schooling and do not participate in the development of their intellectual potential. Children in some families grow up to the sound of music, and are encouraged to develop their creative talents, appreciating the aesthetic dimensions of the realm of *Malchut*. But children in other families are not offered these opportunities.

Both functional and dysfunctional behaviors develop within the context of the family. Children who have grown up in homes where feelings are always hidden may become overly analytical and "live in their heads." This is easier for them than to be in touch with their emotions. Others belong to families that are very supportive of the expression of their emotions. How we deal with our feelings is thus a function of our society and of the dynamics of our family.

The way we relate to people also reflects our society and family rules. Children who grow up in families with authoritarian structures may become adults whose boundaries are impenetrable. Their thinking is often stereotypical, and their ability to achieve intimacy can be severely curtailed by the walls with which they have surrounded themselves. Sometimes they choose spouses who impose their own restrictive rules. Some people who come from such families may become control freaks. But sometimes children react to their authoritarian upbringing by embracing a family style that is too relaxed, and whose boundaries are overly permeable, functioning without adequate defense mechanisms in later life.

Children who grow up in democratic families tend to be flexible in their adult relationships, because they have developed a healthy sense of self and can say no without feeling guilty, confident that self-assertiveness will win them the respect of their spouses and other adults.

In some families, love is unconditional, and their children make lasting commitments. Others are characterized by pressure and stress. Getting love depends on pleasing powerful adults: "If you are good, I'll love you. If you're not good, I'll withhold my love." The children of these families, often fearful of losing love by being assertive, repress their own needs, and some of them become codependent, sustaining their partner's addictive and abusive behaviors. Sometimes children who have experienced the turning on and off of love by dysfunctional parents will become adults with commitment phobias. Consciously or unconsciously, they have come to believe that people simply cannot be trusted to maintain loving, caring, and sharing relationships.

THE SPIRITUAL ROOTS OF UNHAPPINESS

The processes I have described are familiar to anybody with a basic understanding of psychology. What does the Kabbalah add to our understanding of these processes? The doctrine of reincarnation *(gilgul neshamot)* and kabbalistic insights into ego and personality development help explain the spiritual roots of our dysfunctional ways of thinking, feeling, and relating.

THE BURDEN OF PAST-LIFE EXPERIENCES

Brian Weiss's *Many Lives, Many Masters,* Bruce Goldberg's *The Search for Grace,* and my own experience with Betty demonstrate the dramatic and often traumatic effect of past-life experiences. In recent years, despite the skepticism of researchers cited by Antonia Mills and Steven J. Lynn, past-life work has become an important therapeutic tool. Knowledge of who we were, what frustrated us, what fulfilled us, and what caused us suffering in our past lives can illuminate the way we live here and now. Such knowledge is often sufficient to bring us relief and catharsis. I therefore strongly endorse both past-life hypnotherapy and meditative regression.

However, there are many charlatans in the field who are not properly trained in regression techniques. I suggest you do a careful background check on people to whom you have been referred for past-life work before beginning the process. Find out whether they are licensed mental health professionals, and make sure that they are well trained in clinical hypnotherapy. It is also vital for you to know whether they have had extensive experience with past-life regression. Brian Weiss has appended a list of recommended regression hypnotherapists to some of his books.

You should educate yourself about past-life regression before you explore this psychospiritual therapeutic mode. Here are some suggestions: Adrian Finkelstein's *Your Past Lives and the Healing Process: A Psychiatrist Looks at Reincarnation and Spiritual Healing;* Winafred Blake Lucas's *Regression Therapy: A Handbook for Professionals;* and Roger J. Woolger's *Other Lives, Other Selves: A Jungian Psychotherapist Discovers Past Lives.* Brian Weiss's recent *Mirrors of Time: Using Regression for Physical, Emotional, and Spiritual Healing* contains a useful CD and exercises.

EGO DEVELOPMENT: A KABBALISTIC VIEW

But past-life regression is by no means our only option for psychospiritual healing. As you saw in Goldberg's *The Search for Grace,* we are often reincarnated with the people with whom we shared toxic relationships in past lives, and these relationships tend to replay themselves in our current lives. In fact, the reason we come together again is to provide us with fresh opportunities of achieving *tikkun* by mending the dysfunctional ways of being that have crippled and frustrated us in past lives. Understanding why we are unhappy and making changes in our current situation releases us from the cycle of unhappiness.

In chapter 8, I introduced the doctrine of the shattering of the vessels, which is of crucial importance for kabbalistic psychology. According to this doctrine, a number of things occurred as a result of that event, two of which have a direct bearing on the psychology of the Kabbalah.

The first was the creation of evil. You have learned that the Kabbalah refers to the sum total of the powers of evil in the cosmos as the *sitra achra* (the other side). This is in contrast to the **sitra de-kedushah** (the holy side). According to the Kabbalah, the forces of evil parallel the forces of holiness. This means, among other things, that the holy *Sefirot* also have their dark or evil sides. It is clear from

Jung's references to "the shadow" or "the shadow side" of human personality that he understood this principle without necessarily knowing its kabbalistic origin. You will soon see how the kabbalistic notion of the dark side of the holy *Sefirot* affects our understanding of dysfunctional ways of thinking, feeling, and relating.

The Vilna Gaon's discussion of human doubt clarifies the psychospiritual implications of the leeching of the dark *kelipah* energies on to human beings. The very existence of the *kelipot* is the inevitable consequence of their alienation from the Divine. Our own doubts about God's existence mirror this alienation, and are driven by alienated, dark *kelipah* forces. Because we are created in the image of God, when we doubt our authenticity and lose faith in our own innate competencies, it is like doubting the existence of God. This attracts *kelipot* and cripples us psychologically and spiritually. What many psychologists call ego strengths are really only *kelipah* cover-ups for patterns of doubt that undermine our sense of self-worth and frustrate our search for happiness. The examples I shall share with you illustrate exactly how this happens.

Each of these cases shows that our personalities are shaped by the disappointments and/or losses we suffered early in life, and how we interpret the world as a result of those experiences. You will discover that the way we see ourselves, other people, and our world determines our strategy for taking care of ourselves and ensuring that we are going to make it in a dangerous world that is full of people who can hurt and disappoint us.

Many of us equate success with happiness, yet our strategies for success often make us unhappier. I had a colleague in London whose practice was devoted to "affluenza," the problems of highly effective leaders of industry and commerce. All had achieved great financial success. Some were workaholics, some recognized that the cost of their success was family disintegration, and some were guilty about how they had become successful. News of my colleague's specialized practice spread rapidly, and the editors of glossy magazines took notice and ran stories on wealth counseling. Obviously, she had put her finger on a widespread problem.

We met when she signed up for a series of lectures I was giving on psychology and the Kabbalah. At the end of the third or fourth lecture, she remained behind after most of the audience had dispersed. She was clearly excited, and told me that what I had been teaching was the link that she had been missing in her approach to affluenza. She had long recognized that her clients' strategies for success masked profound self-doubt and, sometimes, self-loathing. She now realized that the roots of their problems were as much spiritual as they were psychological.

Strategies for achieving success frequently reflect intrusion of *kelipot* and an increasing imbalance in our inner *sefirah* system. These *kelipot* conceal our true selves, and become the masks or personae that we show the world. They are what we call our egos or personalities. In the course of our development, our inner core becomes so encrusted with these *kelipot* that we can no longer distinguish our true selves from our personae. Our unconscious sense of loss of self is why we feel unhappy, even when we are successful.

LISA'S STORY

Lisa was a rising star in the world of corporate law. She had enrolled in my three-day workshop because she was unhappy and hadn't been able to establish satisfactory relationships. She was fearful of making a commitment to the young man who had recently asked her to marry him. As in most cases, Lisa's earliest memory of disappointment was not dramatic. Her father had been her hero, but was very critical. Her earliest memory was of being rewarded by her father for doing something good. He took her to a drive-in restaurant for ice cream, dressed in his white summer suit. She was so excited that she grabbed the ice cream off the tray and spilled it over him. He was furious. "You're clumsy! You never were any good at anything!" he yelled. This incident had occurred more than twenty years earlier, but Lisa still recalled the hurt and panic she had felt. Her success as an attorney had not diminished the pain.

When asked about other losses or disappointments in her childhood, she recalled an incident that took place a year or two later, when she had just begun elementary school. Her teacher was as critical as her father. Anything less than ten out of ten was unacceptable. This attitude reinforced what she had learned from her father: People would be critical of her unless she was perfect.

When she became a teenager, this view of people was further reinforced. Her friends knew that she was talented, and so they demanded more and more of her. Lisa became the perfect person. She excelled in high school and college, got into the best law school, and then was hired by a prestigious law firm. She had become everything that her father wanted her to be, but, deep inside, she kept hearing her father's comment that she was clumsy and stupid. No matter what she achieved, her "inner critic" filled her with doubt.

The Meaning of Lisa's Story

Lisa's striving for perfection was her defense against self-doubt. Every childhood experience of criticism produced additional perfection defenses. Lisa had covered who she was with the *kelipot* of perfection, the hard shells that would keep her safe, as though she were wearing medieval armor made up of small metal plates.

These shells completely surrounded her, and she was

encumbered by a system of defenses that had been appropriate for a little girl long ago, but had become ineffective and outdated. This intelligent young woman was behaving like a soldier on a modern battlefield in a coat of medieval armor. Her outmoded defenses continued to serve as her strategy for success. If she had been asked to characterize her strengths, she would have used words like *driven, perfectionist,* and *pleaser.* Her friends and colleagues would have used the same words to describe her. Lisa's outdated *kelipot* and strategy for success had become the face she showed the world, her persona. They had also become her personal self-image and ego.

However, beneath her veneer of success and perfection, Lisa was filled with doubt. Her inner critic convinced her that sooner or later she would be exposed as a clumsy, fearful person. She was convinced that the man she loved would reject her as soon as he discovered that she was not really perfect.

Lisa hated having to please everybody else at the expense of pleasing herself. Her sense of inauthenticity was the psychological root of her unhappiness. The spiritual roots of her unhappiness were even deeper. Like all of us, Lisa had come into this world with her personal *sefirah* system in balance, but she had learned that people were critical of her, and had surrounded herself with protective shells. Because analytical intelligence was the key to her formula for success, she had overdeveloped her *Binah.* She had learned that it was easier to "be in her head" than to deal with her feelings. Also, because she felt unsafe, she had overdeveloped her *Gevurah* and, withdrawing into herself, could neither give nor receive love for fear of being rejected. The emotional component of her *Da'at* was also repressed. She was unable to enter into lasting, committed relationships. Ever the pleaser, she had also sacrificed her personal happiness by overdeveloping her *Hod.*

Lisa's *sefirah* system was radically out of sync. The left side of her Tree of Life was overdeveloped and inauthentic. Her *kelipot* had transformed it from "the side of holiness" to the other, dark side. The right side of her Tree of Life, on the other hand, was stunted. She had learned to doubt her intuition, reflecting neglect of her *Chochmah*. She was afraid to love, neglecting her *Chesed* and *Netzach*.

Lisa's healing would depend upon restoring the balance between the left and right sides of her Tree of Life by removing the *kelipot* that were no longer serving her. Their removal and her work on the shadow side of her *sefirah* system would help her embrace the wonderful woman she really was. It would permit her to access her feelings and make the commitment she both wanted and feared.

BARRY'S STORY

Barry saw himself as selfish, manipulative, and ugly. Despite getting almost everything he wanted, he had never experienced a loving relationship, and was extremely depressed. His earliest memory of disappointment was rejection by his mother. She'd taken him to the home of friends whom she wished to impress, and promised to reward him for his good behavior. Barry tried to keep out of trouble by doing nothing that could attract attention. When he eventually felt an urge to go to the bathroom, he did not want to disturb his mother's conversation, so he held himself in. After a while, the pressure on his bladder became unbearable, and he wet his pants and the carpet. He could still remember his mother's reaction. She pretended to be calm and understanding, but punished him severely when they were alone at home. She told him that she was ashamed of him and that if he had really loved her, he would not have embarrassed her. For days after the incident, his mother had been cold and indifferent. He recalled tentatively reaching out to her and telling her how much he loved her. He could still hear her devastating response: "But I can't love you if you're bad."

His mother's behavior was reinforced by his scoutmaster. When the boys did what they were supposed to do, they were rewarded with recognition and affection; but if they failed in competition with other troops, he became angry and distant. Barry learned that you could get what you wanted by giving others what they needed, but his formula for success was Machiavellian. He would give to others only as much as it took to get them to give him what he wanted. When asked how his peers would describe him, he responded that they saw him as a "go-getter," but he was depressed because he knew it was only a matter of time before his truly manipulative and selfish nature would be discovered.

The Meaning of Barry's Story

Barry's mother was the personification of *Netzach* imbalance. She used love to manipulate people who needed her. Barry could have responded to the dark side of his mother's *Netzach* by repressing his own needs and permitting his *Hod* to go out of balance, as Lisa had done. Instead, he chose to become his mother's spiritual clone. His strategy invited the *kelipot* of manipulation. Like the *kelipot* themselves, he leeched on to others, sucking whatever he needed from them through the pretense of genuine caring. But his *kelipot* frustrated any chance of achieving authentic intimacy with a loving partner, because intimacy requires reciprocity and sensitivity. Moreover, Barry doubted himself and the legitimacy of his success. He needed to learn that the defenses that had worked for him in childhood were now, like Lisa's medieval coat of armor, standing in the way of his happiness. Barry's healing would require him to shed his *kelipot,* abandon his success strategy, and rebalance his personal *sefirah* system.

HANNAH'S STORY

Hannah came to see me about her husband's abusive behavior. After taking a full history, developing plans for her to escape to a shelter, and setting up an appointment with her husband, I asked Hannah about her earliest memories of disappointment or loss. She told me that when she was a little child, Rollerblades were the rage. She begged her mom for Rollerblades of her own, and could still hear her response: "Rollerblades are dangerous. You could hurt yourself or even fall in the street and be killed by a car." When Hannah's friends went away to camp, she was not permitted to join them, because her mother was afraid that Hannah would not be safe. She did not even allow Hannah to attend her friends' teen parties, because she was convinced that young men would take advantage of her innocence.

The Meaning of Hannah's Story

Whereas most teenagers would have rebelled against the overprotectiveness of their parents, Hannah learned to view the world as a dangerous place, and doubted that she could manage to survive there on her own. At first, she looked to her parents for protection, and later on to other people. Her formula for survival was to accept authority and become dependable, so that she could safely depend on others. Her friends called her "Miss Reliable." Hannah's strategy had kept her in the abusive relationship with her husband, because she felt protected by strong people. Better to stay with someone who was only sometimes explosive than to risk going it alone. Hannah was all *Hod*, but her personality reflected its dark side. She had become a doormat. Her imbalanced *Sefirot* and cumbersome *kelipot* had disempowered her, and prevented her from developing into an empowered, fully functioning woman.

Our three case examples illustrate how kabbalistic concepts can help us diagnose the roots of our unhappiness. To begin to understand yourself better, you may find the following exercise helpful.

1. List three or four of your earliest memories of loss and disappointment from infancy through adolescence.
2. Describe the way you saw the world and other people as a result of these events.
3. How would your friends and colleagues describe your strengths?
4. How would you describe your character strengths and personality?
5. What is the strategy you devised to survive and achieve success?
6. What doubts does your *kelipah* coat of armor conceal from others?
7. What has been the impact of your strategy on your *sefirah* system?

SUMMARY

Psychologists have long recognized how societal and family values, styles, and rules influence the way children learn to think, deal with emotion, and form relationships. Transgenerational patterns and the consequences of early childhood experiences, hurts, and disappointments have received wide currency in psychological literature.

The Kabbalah adds an important dimension to our understanding of functional and dysfunctional behaviors, suggesting that the roots of unhappiness are spiritual as well as psychosocial, and often go back to unresolved past-life issues and traumas. Qualified regression hypnotherapists have helped clients resolve these issues. However, past-life-regression therapy is not the only way to deal with the spiritual roots of self-defeating ways of thinking, feeling, and relating to other people. We choose the families and social structures into which we are born to learn the lessons we have failed to learn in previous incarnations. Therefore, working with our current life experiences enables us to achieve *tikkun*.

Our early childhood hurts, disappointments, and losses have psychospiritual consequences. In this respect, two aspects of the kabbalistic doctrine of evil have special relevance. First, our *sefirah* energy systems have their dark or shadow side. The way we fashion our lives may throw our *Sefirot* out of balance, replacing positive energy systems with negative patterns. Second, *kelipot* mask our nagging doubts about our competencies and integrity.

Our childhood wounds determine the way in which we see ourselves and the world, and determine the strategies we adopt for survival. Lisa's story shows how repeated criticism of less-than-perfect performance and impatience with her reaction to these criticisms taught her that the most effective strategy in a harsh world was emotional distance and striving for academic and professional perfection. Her friends and associates would have described her high motivation and purposeful behaviors as ego strengths. But success had not brought her happiness. Barry's mother suffered from dark *Netzach* energies, and he became her clone, manipulating all his subsequent relationships while feeling increasingly inauthentic. Hannah's childhood experiences distorted her *Hod* energies, facilitating her tolerance of abuse. The happiness and healing of these people required them to rebalance their *Sefirot* and discard their outmoded *kelipah* defenses.

10

RECLAIMING OUR LIVES

——◆◇◆——

BEYOND INSIGHT

Many clinical outcome studies have shown that an array of psychological problems can be resolved in ten sessions or less, so I decided to learn the techniques of brief psychotherapy at the feet of the master therapists who had developed these dramatic interventions. One of the most important assumptions of this school of psychotherapy is that insight is not enough. I vividly remember the introduction to the seminar I attended at the Mental Research Institute in Palo Alto, California. The instructor described an adult who had been plagued by intractable bed-wetting and, after years of insight therapy, finally understood why he was wetting his bed. But he still wet it. Understanding the origins of a problem is only the beginning of the remedy.

We begin to repair ourselves by taking practical steps to abandon our immature defenses and self-defeating strategies. Then, when we have shed those *kelipot,* we need to observe how these strategies have thrown our personal *sefirah* systems out of balance. Third, we have to restore the balance of our *Sefirot.* Finally, we need to gain access to the light and power within so that we can fulfill our God-given potential and live meaningful, happy lives. This chapter will take us through the first stage of the *tikkun* process.

EXAMINING OUR SCRIPTS FOR LIVING

Many psychologists have written about life scripting. David Feinstein and Stanley Krippner, in *The Mythic Path,* point out that biology and culture play an important role in shaping our personal myths. It is true that we are influenced by our genes, social placement, and so forth. However, transactional analysts such as Eric Berne have argued that we live our lives largely according to the life scripts that we have written during our development to maturity. I have used the following definition of life scripting in working with clients in my clinical practice and in my workshops. Life scripts are "basic, existential decisions about one's life plan made at an early age regarding one's self and others" (Dusay and Dusay, "Transactional Analysis," p. 598). I believe that the first step in our liberation from our *kelipot* is a frank and careful examination of these scripts.

EXERCISE

If you are serious about *tikkun,* you should think about and write down the answers to these questions.

1. When did you first begin to have doubts about your competence and your value as a human being?
2. What event triggered those doubts? It is important that you access your database of memories to hear the voice that first criticized you, and that you remember exactly what was said or done.
3. What did that experience of loss and disappointment tell you about your competence and value as a person?
4. What two or three other events do you remember that rein-

forced these doubts? Can you remember what was said, and by whom?

5. What did those events, critical voices, and undermining actions teach you about people and the world?

6. How did you decide to cope with your insecurity?

7. Can you recall five situations in which your strategy worked and gave you what you needed? Describe them.

8. How would friends and colleagues describe your best qualities and what you do to achieve your goals? Are they describing your strategy accurately?

9. What are you afraid that other people may discover about you?

10. What has your strategy cost you in terms of how you feel about yourself as a person, your missed opportunities, and bungled relationships?

MY PERSONAL TALE

My willingness to share my own failed script for living was always helpful to the participants in my workshops, but there was no way I could have done this without having first rid myself of the *kelipot* that had kept me in my own insecure little world.

When I was training to be a mental health professional, I entered intensive therapy, motivated by my desire to resolve my personal issues and achieve peace of mind. It was not easy for me to go into therapy. I came from a secretive family, and this made it difficult for me to open up to others. I also had a high profile in the community. I was the rabbi of a large congregation and had appeared on radio and television and in print. As a prominent spiritual leader, I had assumed an idealized persona, and was terrified of being unmasked as an insecure, self-doubting individual from a less-than-perfect family.

The last time I saw my father was when I was about four and a half years old. We were told that he had died. Although the family stuck to the story, I gradually came to have nagging doubts about its truthfulness. Ours was a traditional Jewish home. My mother lit Sabbath and festival candles and made those days special for us. When I started going to religious school, I learned that the anniversary of the death of a near and dear one *(yahrzeit)* is marked by lighting a memorial candle at home and saying the **kaddish** prayer in synagogue. But there was no memorial candle or kaddish for my father. In fact, I was never told the Hebrew date of his death. The memorial service for the dead *(yizkor)* is a centerpiece of the three Pilgrim festivals (Passover, Shavuot, and Sukkot) and Yom Kippur. In our synagogue, it was always preceded by an announcement that people whose parents were still alive should leave. I was never asked to remain in synagogue for the *yizkor* service. Although I was usually quick to ask questions about things that puzzled me, I do not recall ever having asked about the lack of ritual observance of my father's death. I must have guessed that there was a dark side to our family history, because no one spoke about my father. Consciously, I put this down to not wanting to upset my mother. Subconsciously, I must have known why the story was taboo. Even though we never heard from my father, and most divorced parents usually maintained some contact with their children, I must have figured out that my parents were divorced. In our circles at that time, nobody could be blamed for a person's death by natural causes, but divorce was a different matter entirely. Good families were supposed to remain intact.

When I told my story, someone asked me why it had never occurred to me that my father might be in jail. I can only suppose that having an imprisoned father was more alien to my experience than divorce. Although divorce was shameful and rare, I knew some divorced families, but had simply never met a family with somebody in jail.

Be that as it may, my children were already teenagers when

I applied for my mother's widow's pension, only to have my suspicions confirmed. The family's lawyer in South Africa wrote me that my parents were divorced shortly after my father moved out. His letter stirred up a whole mix of feelings. I spent the next few years vainly searching for my father, hoping that he was still alive, and discovered in the process that almost everything I had been told about him was untrue. I desperately needed therapy to restore my psychological equilibrium.

My therapists were well trained and tried to help me deal with my anger. One taught me how to nurture my abandoned inner child, and another to identify the parts of my personality that had been affected by the loss, abandonment, and lies, but none was able to help me break with my past. No matter what interventions were attempted, the invisible hand of my father continued to hold me in its grip. Furthermore, none of the interventions addressed the spiritual injuries I had suffered. Even as I was qualifying as a mental health professional, I knew that something was missing in conventional approaches to psychotherapy—including the newly developing psychospiritual interventions.

After working through the process I'm about to share with you, I was finally able to validate myself as a person and tell my story with no sense of shame.

The first thing I learned about the world and the people in it was that they were scary. I also learned that I would always have to take care of myself because nobody else would. There was no money for tutoring and nobody at home to teach me boyhood skills.

I vividly recall the last occasion the boy next door beat me up. I can still feel the pressure of his headlock, but I also remember disassociating myself from the pain and taking careful note of every move he made. That beating became my manual for self-defense.

Sports were big in South Africa. If you did not make the elementary school soccer team, you could not possibly win the respect of your peers. I did not make the team, and so I had to figure out a way of learning to play the game other than by kicking a ball against the wall at home. I created a soccer team of my own, designing the uniforms for the players, and even organizing an entire soccer league. Within a year, I was on the elementary school team.

There were two ways of making it big in high school. You either excelled at sports or academically. Academics provided more opportunities than rugby. You did not have to be lightning fast or powerfully built to succeed. I became an academic overachiever. It was mandatory to take six subjects to matriculate. I took seven and became the school's valedictorian.

I stuttered when I spoke in public, but a teacher recognized that this was due to my lack of confidence. Over my protests, she placed me on the school debating team and forced me to speak in public. Before long, the stuttering stopped, and I won the Speaker's Cup.

My family could not afford the cost of a college education, so I applied for and won a scholarship. Students were required to have no more than three full majors, but I received special dispensation from the academic senate to major in four subjects. Simultaneously, I became a national leader of my youth movement, and to help the family finances, also had three part-time jobs. In my senior year, notwithstanding all the other things that were going on, I enrolled as a freshman in rabbinic school.

I married very young, and was ordained as a rabbi and gained master's and doctoral degrees in philosophy—all in a fairly short period of time. I became the senior rabbi of a major congregation and the youngest full professor at the University of Natal. Once again, I was doing two full-time jobs, proving to myself and the world that I could succeed in meeting every challenge and excel at every task.

If you had asked my friends and colleagues to describe me, they would have said that I was *self-motivated, driven, ambitious, intellectual, rational, analytical,* and *accomplished.* They would have seen me just the way I wanted them to see me. My successes reflected my life script. My strategies had worked.

But every time I presented a paper at an international meeting, I was afraid that somebody would discover that my success had been a fluke, and that I was not nearly as bright as I appeared to be. I had also become less and less happy with what I was doing and the way I was doing it. I was making a very good living, and I had achieved a high level of recognition and admiration, both as a rabbi and as an academic. So why was I unhappy?

TAKING RESPONSIBILITY

By now, it should be clear why I asked you to examine your life script, and why I have gone public with my own. If we are honest in the way we examine our life scripts, we must reach one startling conclusion: *We must take sole responsibility for how we have lived our lives.*

- *We have written our own scripts.* Nobody else—not our fathers, our mothers, or our teachers—wrote those scripts.
- *Our interpretation of the world and the people in it is also our very own.* We write our scripts according to our own view of the world.
- *Our strategies for success are our own.* Nobody told me to become a workaholic, an overly busy rabbi, and a successful academic in order to prove my worth. It was my own way of

making a somebody out of a lonely, frightened, abandoned child. Do you remember the stories in chapter 9? Nobody told Lisa that her path to success depended on pleasing others. Nobody told Barry that the way to get what he wanted was by exploiting other people's weaknesses. Nobody told Hannah that she needed others to keep her safe, even if her strategy would sometimes bring her great pain.

⊙ *The doubts we have about ourselves are our own.* We call our insecure feelings about our weaknesses "self-doubts." When we fear that other people will come to doubt our competence and value as human beings, we are projecting our own doubts onto them. They don't doubt us. We doubt ourselves.

Before we can achieve happiness, we have to accept responsibility for our unhappiness and for the *kelipot,* the childish, outmoded defenses we continue to use. But it's not easy for us to do so. We've grown up in a culture of victimization. We've learned to blame others for what we've done to ourselves. Lawsuits against tobacco companies typify our victim culture. It's difficult to believe that most people are not aware of the health hazards of smoking. Nevertheless, some people who have made themselves ill by continuing to smoke do not take responsibility for the consequences of their choice. They blame the tobacco companies—and juries, buying into the culture of blame, have rewarded them with generous sums of money.

It has now been well established that schizophrenia is a psychoneurological disorder, a function of the activity of our neurotransmitters. It is not primarily connected to psychosocial conditions. But before its neurological basis became known, therapists blamed it on parents, suggesting that dysfunctional mothers created schizophrenia-producing double-bind, no-win conflict situations for their children. Unfortunately, some psychotherapists persist in relieving their clients of responsibility for their dysfunctional behaviors by shifting blame to their parents.

Tikkun demands that we shed our victim mentality. As long as we are content to blame others for our unhappiness, we simply cannot go forward. Shifting responsibility to others for our choices is counter to the Judaic ethic. It also contradicts the basic kabbalistic principle that God deliberately created a world in which there is evil to enable us to choose between good and evil. Our responsible choices contribute either to the further disintegration of the cosmos or to its *tikkun,* and to our personal regression or growth. We are not only responsible for the choices we make in the here and now, but also for the critical choices we made before we were born. Each new *gilgul* (reincarnation) is an opportunity to undo the errors of the past and to learn new lessons. To ensure that the environment into which we are born will be best suited for the challenges of the new *gilgul,* we actually choose our parents, our bodies, our families, and the most important people with whom to relate. Because we make these choices ourselves, it makes no sense to blame others for how we have scripted and shall continue to script our lives.

ACHIEVING COMPLETION

Our scripts begin with traumatic memories of early losses and/or disappointments. According to our scripts, our parents, teachers, and peers are responsible for the hurts that shape our lives. Shifting responsibility from others to ourselves requires us to take steps whose effectiveness has been demonstrated by the successful transformational work of the Landmark Forum. My own story validates this process.

MY PERSONAL TALE *(continued)*

I was already in my forties when I saw documents confirming that my mother was a divorcée rather than a widow. I needed to talk to my father and tell him how upset I was that he had never made any effort to contact me and find out who I was and how I was doing. I needed to express the anger and pain I had felt for decades, but I also wanted him to know that I did not blame him for the way I had subsequently interpreted my world, scripted my life, and strategized my success.

However, the detectives I hired in three countries came up with nothing. He had disappeared without a trace. So I decided to write him a long letter, telling him how hurt I had been by his sudden disappearance and how it felt to be abandoned and without a male role model. I wrote angrily about his failure to contact me to say he was alive and cared about me, and described the secret shame I had felt about our family lies about his death.

After this emotional outpouring, I described what I had done to succeed. What I told him was far more detailed than the account I gave earlier, but I made it clear that I knew that I was solely responsible for having become an unhappy overachiever.

I could not send the letter to my father, nor could I place it on his grave, for I did not know where he was buried. But I had seen one or two photographs of him, so I pictured him sitting with me at the table, and I read my letter to him.

The experience was cathartic. I wept as I read, but was relieved that I had been able to share my feelings with my father without blaming him for how I had fashioned my life. The past had been completed. The pattern of anger and blame was broken, and I was free to move on.

My letter to my father is only one model for completing the past. The best way is to speak face-to-face with the person who caused your initial hurt. This offers that person an opportunity to say that he or she had not intended to hurt you. However, in many cases, the hurt was deliberate and a reflection of the person's own dysfunction. Engaging such a person is a tough assignment, and the odds are high that he or she will become angry or defensive. Most people are unable to own up to their unacceptable behaviors, but you must not allow yourself to be drawn into a new cycle of accusation and counteraccusation. The point of the encounter is not to ask for forgiveness or to elicit a confession. It is simply to give you an opportunity to say precisely what happened, and to make clear that you are not blaming him or her for how you scripted your life thereafter. The entire purpose of the exercise is to allow you to distinguish between the memory of hurtful events and how you chose to fashion your life as a result.

USEFUL PREPARATIONS FOR COMPLETION

⊙ *The Empty Chair.* Gestalt therapy pioneer Fritz Perls introduced the empty chair technique. Clients imagine that someone with whom they have issues is occupying an empty chair in the office or in their home. They speak to that person as if he or she were actually present. The empty chair technique is particularly effective for reparenting the inner child. Adults who were neglected or abused as children imagine themselves occupying the empty chair as the little children they once were. They offer the children comfort, nurturing, support, love, and validation. Although, at first glance, this technique appears to be contrived, it is very cathartic. The empty chair is also a useful vehicle for dealing with bereavement. The deceased person is imagined in the empty chair and spoken to about repressed angers, disappointments, lost opportunities and dreams, and other unfinished business.

⊙ *Role-Play*. Many people do not know how to translate what they have learned in therapy into real-life situations, and are likely to be anxious about how they might respond to the unexpected reactions of the people they have feared since childhood. The therapist or any other intelligent person can assume the role of the toxic father, mother, or teacher in the safety of the office or the person's own home. If people are paralyzed by the simulated negative reactions of those who have hurt them, the therapist or role-play partner can model appropriate responses. It is also useful for people who are preparing for completion to play the role of the feared person, because they can best anticipate his or her negative or angry reactions. If this technique is used, the therapist or partner can model appropriate ways of responding to the negativity. Role-playing is also an effective tool in self-assertiveness and self-esteem training, forgiveness, and couples issues. I recommend to interested readers the therapy summary on behavior rehearsal in *Behavior Therapy,* by John C. Masters, Thomas G. Burish, Steven D. Hollon, and David C. Rimm. Of course, the pioneering works on psychodrama by Jacob L. Moreno still command attention.

In the question period after one of my lectures, I was asked about the morality of confronting a parent with his or her hurtful behavior or attitude. How can you respectfully say to a parent, "You are a bad person. You did such and such to me" without violating the Fifth Commandment, the prohibition against disrespect for parents? I answered that most parents who have hurt us are not wicked, but are probably ignorant or flawed. They are likely to be transmitters of dysfunctional patterns in their own families of origin, or may be acting out the effects of a previous incarnation.

I also told the questioner that if she had first convinced herself that her unhappiness was her own doing, she would have been able to engage her mother without bitterness, and that her feelings were caused by her own self-image of being a victim. Once she had dropped that image, she could encounter her parents without hostility.

I added that the biblical commandment to "honor thy father and thy mother" *(kibbud av)* is different from **shibbud av,** being controlled by parents. As long as victims have others to blame for their unhappiness, they give them control of their lives. Face-to-face completion with a parent, thereby taking personal responsibility for one's life, is a cathartic method of reclaiming our lives by removing the veto we permitted our parent to have on who we are and how we live.

Sometimes, however, a face-to-face conversation is simply too difficult, because we anticipate a hostile reaction or fear for our safety. A telephone conversation may be easier. However, even a telephone conversation of this kind may be beyond us. I have said that most people are not bad, but there are exceptions. Some people's patterns of abuse and sadistic delight are undeniable. Any direct contact with them can be toxic. In such cases, a detailed letter like the one I wrote my father will also work. If this is your situation, picture the person who hurt you sitting in front of you and read your letter aloud. Reading the letter at the graveside of someone who hurt you brings a particularly powerful release.

It does not matter what method of completion you choose. What does matter is that your description of what happened between you is only the first part of the communication. The most important part is taking full responsibility for what you did as a result. You must state clearly that your interpretation of the world and of the people in it was your own, and that it had nothing to do with the person who hurt you.

If you were able to engage the person who hurt or disappointed you, I recommend that you write a detailed account of your conversation. However, whether you speak directly or read a letter, as I did, sharing your feelings with someone you trust and recording those feelings is likely to help you. After taking responsibility for my life script and failed strategies, I shared my feelings in a transformational seminar with participants who were going through similar completion processes. The experience was truly liberating.

11

REBALANCING OUR *SEFIROT*
OF COGNITION

COMPLETION IS ONLY THE BEGINNING

Completing our past toxic relationships and freeing ourselves from the psychological control of people who have hurt or disappointed us is liberating and empowering. But completion is not, by itself, a magic bullet for healing damaged souls and achieving *tikkun.* Much more needs to be done.

The most insidious psychospiritual effect of our failed strategies for successful survival is the damage they do to our personal *sefirah* systems. The damage is twofold. First, our *Sefirot* are thrown out of balance. Second, our holy side is replaced by the dark side. Our *Sefirot* no longer function as channels for divine energy, but for self-defeating ways of thinking, being, and relating.

A contemporary therapist, Dorothy S. Becvar, has reminded us of the connection between healing, wholeness, and holiness. "Holiness," she writes in *Soul Healing,* "is the essence of healing, which means to manifest wholeness in spirit and bring it into our bodies, our families, our communities, our world."

But rebalancing our *Sefirot* is hard work. This and the next three chapters offer psychological and spiritual techniques for rebalancing our *Sefirot.*

Earlier, you learned that *Chochmah* is a spiritual building block of the *Neshamah,* the antenna that receives wisdom from the higher realms of our individual and collective souls. It is our opening to inspiration, creativity, and intuition, and is responsible for what some people call right-brain activity.

Western society, by this popular definition, is left-brain oriented. From earliest childhood, we are trained to think linearly, logically, and analytically. Math and science are emphasized, and critical thinking is a required course in many graduate schools. Sometimes this is taken to extremes. I know a young man who is a gifted poet inclined to mysticism, but when he applied for admission to the graduate programs for poets, he worked hard to make sure that he would also receive a good grade in the math section of the Graduate Record Examination (GRE). What more striking proof can there be for Western overemphasis on logical skills? We are taught to trust only things we can analyze and prove scientifically.

The effect of this orientation is a distrust of intuition and phenomena that do not fit comfortably into logical categories. We have been brought up to distrust our gut feelings and be suspicious of spontaneity. Yet, as I have pointed out, even scientific breakthroughs are the result of intuition, and great art and music are inspired. Therefore, living by logic alone, while repressing inspiration and intuition, is like driving a car with only half its cylinders firing.

But "artsy," disorganized people who have neglected their left-brain functions are also driving with half their cylinders shut down, because their *Binah* requires unblocking. People who fail to synthesize their *Chochmah* and *Binah* in *Da'at* also need *sefirah* rebalancing, because disorders of our cognitive *Sefirot* are interrelated.

In addition to inhibiting our cognitive potential, some of us have to contend with other effects of our self-defeating strategies on our *Sefirot* of cognition. The following examples will give you an idea of some ways to unblock and rebalance the *Sefirot* of cognition.

THERAPEUTIC STRATEGIES

EDNA'S STORY

Edna enrolled in my workshop because she was overly analytical and could not get in touch with her feelings. She was always in her head and never in her heart. She had grown up in a very orderly home. Her parents could not stand any mess, and were hard on her if she did not clean up after herself and put all her toys neatly into the labeled drawers where they belonged. Edna loved arts and crafts and delighted in drawing and making paper cutouts before her parents returned from work. But if her parents came home early and found traces of paint or paper in her room, she would be scolded for such "babyish" activities and for being so messy. Edna soon learned not to waste her time on "stupid" things that produced no immediate payoff, and that success was tied to neatness and structure. When she grew up, she became a first-class manager. No files were ever lost in her office, and nobody in her department was permitted to clutter their desks. She was rewarded well for her efficiency. Edna was miserable, and was paid to be miserable.

The Meaning of Edna's Story

It was clear that Edna's cognitive *sefirah* system was out of balance. She had overly developed her *Binah* to avoid the negative consequences of messy, spontaneous creativity, and the price of her success was her attenuated *Chochmah*.

Repairing Edna's Sefirot of Cognition

Edna agreed to use the telephone for completion with her parents, and was pleasantly surprised by the outcome. She also enrolled in an ongoing program of therapy that was offered as an adjunct to my workshops. In addition to our weekly therapeutic dialogue, these were the main interventions we tried.

- *Gardening.* Edna loved going to flower shows and visiting botanical gardens, with their manicured lawns and neatly arranged, color-coordinated flower beds. These things seemed to appeal to her sense of order and her repressed aesthetic sensibilities. I suggested she take up gardening, which is naturally messy. The best-tended gardens produce weeds, and clean hands become grubby. Edna had found something she could do without hearing the critical voices of her parents.
- *Painting.* I recommended that Edna enroll in art classes, preferably those that required her to dirty her hands, such as sculpture, ceramics, and finger painting. I encouraged her to create a small studio in her home and to supplement her formal art instruction with spontaneous, "messy" creativity. She was to report how she felt as she became increasingly engaged in this project, and how she dealt with the reactions of her husband and children to her new hobby.
- *Programmed Spontaneity.* I asked Edna and her husband to make a commitment to do one unusual thing for each other every week. They were not to discuss the surprise ahead of time. Each was to guess what it had been, if it had not been too obvious. The important thing was that the activity should be uncharacteristic of their previous patterns of interaction.
- *Daily Meditation.* Edna set aside twenty minutes a day for meditation. I recorded a number of guided meditations for her use at home and recommended Rabbi Aryeh Kaplan's *Jewish Meditation.* She also purchased a number of meditation CDs that would help her to develop her *Chochmah.* I shall suggest a guided meditation to you later in this chapter.

ISAAC'S STORY
***

Isaac had grown up in a family that was rationally oriented, tightly structured, and emotionally repressed. "Men don't cry," his father would remind his son. The family strategy for dealing with disappointment would be to plan different ways of handling similar situations in the future. Isaac's parents would analyze the children's problems at family discussions, and help them to work out more adaptive solutions. The family rule was planned adaptation, without allowing feelings to get in the way of practical ways of dealing with pain and disappointments. At school, Isaac became the class "fixer." He would analyze problems and propose workable solutions. Isaac's strategy for transforming his struggle for survival into a winning formula for success eventually paid off in the corporate world. His solution-oriented approaches to problems earned him rapid promotion. He was soon at the top of the heap, intolerant of the weaknesses of people who worked for him, and willing to ax nonproductive associates. Isaac's career was successful, his children were well behaved, and his family was an extension of his corporate success, but he was miserable. What did his wife mean by her tearful comment that he had made her feel invisible? Why did the people who admired him most seem to like him least? Why was he afraid that he would be fired in the same way that he had dismissed others?

The Meaning of Isaac's Story

Isaac had come to epitomize the dark side of *Binah.* Hardnosed analysis had replaced his ability to acknowledge and deal with pain and disappointment. Criticism of others and nononsense problem solving had become a substitute for intimate sharing. No wonder his wife claimed she didn't really know him. He didn't know himself, and had begun to realize that he was raising arrogant, alienated children who were his clones.

Repairing Isaac's Sefirot *of Cognition*

After working through a difficult completion process with his parents, Isaac committed himself to regular therapy. We tried the following interventions.

⊙ *Reparenting the Inner Child.* When I was dealing with my personal abandonment issues after my family's secret was revealed, my therapist suggested that I try reparenting my inner child. She told me to bring a photograph of myself as a little boy and put it on a pillow. I was to embrace the pillow and imagine that it was the little boy in the picture. I was to cuddle the little boy and tell him how much I loved him. I protested that I was far too rational to engage in such an absurd exercise. My therapist referred me to gestalt therapy literature, and asked me not to allow my overanalytical mind-set to block the healing process. We reached a compromise. I would not make a fool of myself by doing what she wanted in front of her, but I agreed to try it in the privacy of my own home. I was amazed at what happened. I soon got past the strangeness of imagining that the pillow I was cuddling was myself as a little boy. My tears began to flow as I acknowledged the boy's pain, loneliness, and fears, and reassured him that I loved him. Believe it or not, reparenting my own inner child had made me feel much better about myself, and had opened me to a world of feelings I had long disowned.

When my therapist saw the dramatic changes, she recommended that I read Hal Stone and Sidra Winkelman's work on voice dialogue. I recommend it to my readers.

I told this story of my inner child work to Isaac. His initial reaction was exactly the same as mine, but he agreed to set aside five minutes every day alone, and report what happened. Isaac's reparenting of his inner child had the same effect as mine. The rebalancing of his cognitive *Sefirot* had begun. He was now ready to become aware of his feelings and rid himself of his dysfunctional *Binah* activities.

⦿ *Role-Play.* By assuming the roles of his employers, employees, wife, children, and clients, with me "playing" Isaac in the dialogue, Isaac was able to experience the impact of his insensitive management style on others.

⦿ *The Empty Chair.* It was now no great leap for Isaac to experiment with this gestalt technique, this time in my office. He was able to imagine his inner child in the empty chair, dialogue with him, and, in time, encounter the disowned parts of his own personality. You can refresh your memory about the empty chair technique by reviewing page 166.

⦿ *Emotional Journaling.* After Isaac had read David D. Burns and Aaron Beck's *Feeling Good,* I asked him to pay attention to even the least sign of emotion and to record his feelings in a daily journal, in columns, under the headings *Time, Emotion, Trigger,* and *Response.* Here are some examples from Isaac's feeling journal.

Emotion: Fear. *Trigger:* His wife's threat to leave him following a major blowup. *Response:* Buying his wife a new convertible to divert her from her anger.

Emotion: Feelings of loss. *Trigger:* Seeing another couple in excited and loving communication about unimportant little things. *Response:* Unsuccessful attempt to engage his wife in the same kind of conversation.

Emotion: Panic. *Trigger:* Warning by his corporate directors that he was responsible for their profit downturn. *Response:* Failed attempts to strategize effective business alternatives.

Emotion: Depression. *Trigger:* Evidence of the disintegration of his world. *Reaction:* Self-pity and hopelessness.

   Isaac was learning to tune in to his heart and accept the limitations of his usual rational, linear strategies for success.

He did not do the exercises in Burns's *The Feeling Good Handbook,* because we were reviewing his emotional journaling in session on a regular basis. However, I do recommend this handbook to readers who would like to learn emotional journaling on their own.

◉ *Systematic Desensitization.* Behavior modification pioneer Joseph Wolpe *(The Practice of Behavior Therapy)* observed that it is difficult to experience positive and negative feelings simultaneously. He trained his patients to relax deeply and put themselves in a place of tranquillity and well-being. He then asked them to list the things that scared them most, starting with their smallest fear and moving through the list to the scariest. While they were enjoying the effects of deep relaxation, often with a soothing musical background, he instructed them to think over and over again about the thing that was lowest on their anxiety list. It did not take long for this fear to be extinguished. They were then asked to repeat the process, moving slowly upward through the list of anxiety triggers. I asked Isaac to make his own hierarchy of fears and anxieties. Most of the items on his list were taken from his feelings journal. His anxieties were gradually extinguished, and he was able to own his feelings without fear.

◉ *Couples Therapy.* In the safety of my office, Isaac's wife was able to talk about her loneliness and the anger of their children at Isaac's distant, "know-it-all," and autocratic style of family management. I asked Isaac to share with his wife the feelings and fears he had recorded in his journal. He thought he would look foolish and weak, but, to his surprise, she was visibly moved by and delighted in his newfound vulnerability. Communication training helped them deal with the difficult issues that had so long been swept under the rug. Scheduling "surprises" and weekly romantic "dates" without the children introduced intimacy and spontaneity into their relationship. Their regular participation in musical and theatrical presentations, seminars, and workshops reawakened in him his repressed aesthetic sensibilities.

For the Record

Isaac's children were astonished by the changes. Their dad was no longer dismissive of their feelings and foibles. Their input into family discussions was welcomed and their feelings validated. The family dynamic had changed completely.

LINDA'S STORY

Linda came to see me for help with her disorganized and impetuous ways of being. Her parents were nonconforming holdovers from the flower-power generation of the 1960s. Doors were never closed, and privacy was not respected. All Linda's foibles had been indulged. Her whining about her repeated failures in arithmetic, math, and science convinced her parents that she would develop much better with home-schooling, with an emphasis on arts, music, theater, and dance. Linda quickly learned that she could succeed by complaining that she didn't want to be like other kids.

Her strategy was "artsy" nonconformism. Unfortunately for Linda, her parents died without leaving her an inheritance. She moved from job to job, place to place, home to home, and relationship to relationship. She was unsuccessful at selling her art and at theatrical and dance auditions. Her self-esteem hit rock bottom.

The Meaning of Linda's Story

Linda's cognitive *Sefirot* were clearly out of balance. Her *Chochmah* had become a shadow of itself. In addition, her neglect of her rational faculties had attenuated her *Binah*. Her impetuous